Shakespeare's Sonnets and Poems:
A Very Short Introduction

VERY SHORT INTRODUCTIONS are for anyone wanting a stimulating and accessible way into a new subject. They are written by experts, and have been translated into more than 45 different languages.

The series began in 1995, and now covers a wide variety of topics in every discipline. The VSI library now contains over 500 volumes—a Very Short Introduction to everything from Psychology and Philosophy of Science to American History and Relativity—and continues to grow in every subject area.

Very Short Introductions available now:

Available soon:

For more information visit our website

www.oup.com/vsi/

Jonathan F. S. Post

SHAKESPEARE'S SONNETS AND POEMS

A Very Short Introduction

OXFORD
UNIVERSITY PRESS

OXFORD

UNIVERSITY PRESS

Great Clarendon Street, Oxford, OX2 6DP,
United Kingdom

Oxford University Press is a department of the University of Oxford.
It furthers the University's objective of excellence in research, scholarship,
and education by publishing worldwide. Oxford is a registered trade mark of
Oxford University Press in the UK and in certain other countries

First edition published in 2017

Impression: 2

Published in the United States of America by Oxford University Press
198 Madison Avenue, New York, NY 10016, United States of America

British Library Cataloguing in Publication Data
Data available

Library of Congress Control Number: 2017937424

ISBN 978-0-19-871757-7

Printed in Great Britain by
Ashford Colour Press Ltd, Gosport, Hampshire

To Ben, Dylan, Allyson, Luke,
Griffin, and Johnny

Contents

Contents

Acknowledgements

In writing this *Shakespeare's Sonnets and Poems: A Very Short Introduction*, I have accumulated a surprisingly large number of debts. During a time of barbarous incivilities on so many fronts, it is a pleasure to thank the following: A. R. Braunmuller, Colin Burrow, Hannah Crawforth, Alice Fulton, John Kerrigan, Elizabeth Scott-Baumann, and Stephen Yenser; the many scholars who contributed essays to the *Oxford Handbook of Shakespeare's Poetry*; my Shakespeare students at UCLA, undergraduate and graduate alike; that trio of administrative wizards and librarians in the UCLA English Department, Jeanette Gilkison, Hillary Gordon, and Lynda Tolly; Kathryn Ballsun of the UCLA Friends of English; and three colleagues who read the manuscript from different perspectives but with care and insight: Stephen Dickey, Kimberly Hedlin, and Curtis Whitaker. I also want to thank the Academic Senate and the Council on Research at UCLA for continuing to support my research over the years. Jenny Nugee has been a delight to work with at Oxford University Press. As in the past, Susan Gallick is this book's 'onlie begetter'. To times in hope, I dedicate it to a new generation of Shakespeare readers in the making.

List of illustrations

Chapter 1
Poet and playwright

Origins, centre, circumference

Unbeknownst to me at the time, this *Shakespeare's Sonnets and Poems: A Very Short Introduction* had its origins in an invitation to give a Valentine's Day talk in a posh Beverly Hills garden setting. At such a time as this, I thought, who could be better to invoke than Shakespeare? Had he not authored some of the most famous lines about love in the English language, especially in the Sonnets: from the exquisitely simple query, 'Shall I compare thee to a summer's day?' (18), to the resonantly firm command, 'Let me not to the marriage of true minds / Admit impediments' (116)?

As it turns out, Shakespeare has little to say directly about Valentine's Day—and even less of the sentimental sort often found on greeting cards celebrating this largely commercial venture. Ophelia's song in *Hamlet*, 'Tomorrow is Saint Valentine's day' (4.5.48), is probably the most memorable instance, her plaintive recollection of the occasion reflecting her descent into madness in the tale of the deflowered maid. But on the general topic of love, and its varieties, Shakespeare is nearly unstoppable, as was my variably seasoned audience on that day. Not only does love finger its incessant way through Shakespeare's plays, the Comedies (and late Romances), as we might well expect, and all the Tragedies, leaving its traces in the urge toward marriage or the drive to death, and at least some of the Histories, with their complex social and political concerns, but love receives its maximal concentration in Shakespeare's poems.

To that end, Emerson's comment, made in reference to the Sonnets, seems right on target with regard to the poems, for what is most striking about the poems too 'is the assimilating power of passion that turns all things to its own nature'. Yes, all things. Venus can think of nothing but seducing Adonis, while Lucrece, the greedy object of Tarquin's lust, understands her identity only as an inseparable, inviolable condition of lust's opposite: her chastity. So, too, the unnamed maid in *A Lover's Complaint*, like the Ancient Mariner, is destined to keep repeating the tale of her vanquishment, enveloped by it. Only the unnamed lovers eulogized in 'The Phoenix and Turtle' might be seen as escaping the power of passion's predicaments, in their case, through a marriage of true minds. They are, as is the Phoenix, exceptional by nature, beyond Reason, in fact.

Most readers will have a general sense of a sonnet, but what do we mean when we refer to Shakespeare's *poems*, as opposed to, say, the general topic of Shakespeare's *poetry*? The latter term is often invoked to describe, rather loosely, the generally flowery—or poetic—nature of Shakespeare's language: rich in imagery and metaphor, lofty in sentiment, eloquent in address, as stirring as a drumroll and deep as a well. Responses like these often underlie or bolster Shakespeare's being called, as he so often is, the greatest poet in the English language, and they are applicable to works written by him for both stage and page. I, too, find Shakespeare rich, eloquent, stirring, and deep, but our focus in this *Very Short Introduction* is on the relatively small group of poems never collected together in Shakespeare's lifetime but, except in one case, all published as separate books during his life. In chronological order, these are the two narrative poems, *Venus and Adonis* (1593) and *The Rape of Lucrece* (1594), 'The Phoenix and Turtle', which initially appeared as part of a collection of poems called *Love's*

Martyr (1601), and the *Sonnets* (1609), to which is appended, with its own separate title page, the narrative poem known as *A Lover's Complaint*.

Not a large body of writing, to be sure, although the 154 Sonnets represent something of a record for sonnet collections of the period written in English, to say nothing about the volumes of commentary they have inspired. There have been attempts to expand the boundaries of the canon, especially in the later 17th century, as Shakespeare's reputation as a local Stratford writer grew, to include little squibs and lapidary verse. Attempts continue to this day. The reward for discovering a new Shakespeare poem is not quite akin, financially, to uncovering a new Vermeer or Rembrandt, but it has led many a scholar to propose possibilities that have, after later consideration, seemed premature. If popular sentiment only were our guide, the poem with the greatest likelihood of sticking is the sturdy 'Epitaph on Himself', carved on the stone slab covering his grave in heavily trampled Holy Trinity Church in Stratford-upon-Avon. It bears the warning, so far effective:

> Good friend, for Jesus' sake forbear
> To dig the dust enclosèd here.
> Blessed be the man that spares these stones,
> And cursed be he that moves my bones.

Professional Shakespeareans might lean in a different direction, perhaps toward 'Verses on the Stanley Tomb at Tong', but since none of the poems later attributed to Shakespeare is of incontrovertible authority and most are brief and conventional, they will not figure in this book. Nor will more than passing reference be made to poems that appear in plays, like the famous sonnet in *Romeo and Juliet* beginning 'If I profane with my unworthiest hand' (1.5.90). A fuller discussion, depending as it does on understanding their dramatic context, would take us far afield from the major concerns of this study.

Nonetheless, small in number though the poems seem with respect to the thirty-six plays Shakespeare is generally assumed to have authored (thirty-nine, including those in which he collaborated with others), they are still not disproportionately small when compared to, say, the contemporaries with whom Shakespeare is most frequently compared: Christopher Marlowe and Ben Jonson. Marlowe's non-dramatic work consisted primarily of translations (from Lucan and Ovid), one narrative poem, of considerable flair and fame, *Hero and Leander*, and a single pastoral lyric, much imitated in its day ('The Passionate Shepherd to his Love'). But Marlowe's current reputation rests mainly on the six plays he wrote for the stage, the best known being *Doctor Faustus*, *Tamburlaine*, Parts I and 2, *The Jew of Malta,* and *Edward II*. Jonson made a stronger bid in his day to be known as a Poet (in capital letters), which he demonstrated in mid-career when he published his *Works* in 1616. The Folio book included two important collections of verse (*Epigrams* and *The Forest*), and a number of court masques and entertainments alongside the nine plays; but the overall effect of the volume is to underscore the social function of Jonson's authority as a successful writer on many fronts: at court, in the theatre, on the street, and among the wealthy.

Shakespeare never aspired to such authorial inclusiveness as Jonson. Indeed, perhaps not much to authorship at all, if we accept, as many scholars including this one do not, the popular version of him as someone who just got lucky with words, warbling 'his native wood notes wild'. Like Marlowe, Shakespeare was initially drawn to the theatre, from which activity he turned to writing poems as occasion, need, and ambition invited or required, especially when the theatres were closed because of the plague. But Marlowe was himself only a partial model for Shakespeare. He died too young to influence more than Shakespeare's early career and not the Sonnets at all. Like Jonson, Marlowe left that page blank. (Or nearly blank in the case of Jonson, a professed disdainer of sonnets who managed to squeeze out a few.) For contemporary examples of this kind, Shakespeare had to turn in a different direction: to the works of slightly older humanist courtiers such as Sir Philip Sidney and Edmund Spenser. These poets imagined themselves in a line with influential European authors, particularly Francis Petrarch, a line Shakespeare continued but with a distinct swerve when it came to writing sonnets of his own.

Shakespeare's double occupation

In many regards, the single most important point about Shakespeare's double life as poet and playwright is how fruitful this generic crisscrossing was for him artistically. His poems, the narrative poems for certain, but the Sonnets as well, have an earthy, psychological, and theatrical element to them rarely found among his more exclusively elite poetic contemporaries like Spenser and Samuel Daniel. Take the narrative poems: vivid with imagery, intensely dramatic in their attention to dialogue and bodily movement, they sometimes seem as if Shakespeare were imagining on the page an action being staged—or perhaps one that couldn't be staged except in the mind—and then setting it down but, in this case, using a complicated verse pattern. At the end of *Lucrece*, for instance, Brutus and his fellow Romans, like actors, gather around and swear a great oath to Lucrece's body, a 'bleeding body', we're then told in the final stanza, that is not only shown around Rome for all the public to see but also seen by us, in the mind's eye, as the poem's closing image. Likewise, Sonnet 23 begins,

> As an unperfect actor on the stage,
> Who with his fear is put besides his part,
> Or some fierce thing replete with too much rage,
> Whose strength's abundance weakens his own heart[.]

So precise is the comparison between the stage struck actor and the star struck lover that the conceit seems imaginable only for someone who has spent serious time in the theatre.

At the same time, the plays are filled not just with poetry but with poems, verse forms, especially sonnets, lyrics, songs (artful ones as well as 'snatches'), and dirges or epitaphs. They are written with an ear to rhyme, sometimes to close off a scene and occasionally, as in *Richard II*, to establish a ceremonial, archaic feel, against which the new political regime in that play is measured. One way to understand Shakespeare's extraordinary growth as a writer, in fact, is to note the loosening of the spoken line in the theatre, and the greater freedom taken with stress patterns, shared lines, and the like. *The Two Gentlemen of Verona* (*c.*1591) and *The Tempest* (1611), separated by twenty years, are miles apart in this regard. *Two Gentlemen* feels in places as if the speeches had been cut from a page of Elizabethan printed verse and handed to an actor to make with them as he will (and it was always a 'he' in the pre-Restoration theatre). The pentameter lines are often uniform in number and frequently end-stopped, with the length of the ten-syllable line frequently corresponding exactly with the sense. Prospero, in *The Tempest*, is made from nearly opposite clay. Notoriously long-winded at the outset, he seems to improvise on stage, from one hypermetrical line to the next, as if hearing himself speak, listening to the sound of his own thinking.

Shakespeare's poems cannot be said to exhibit the same movement toward expressive freedom or growth, although the interior thinking of the Sonnets seems distinguished by the kind of private ruminations we find, say, in Richard II's final soliloquy, or in Hamlet's continual musings. This difference, in part, is a result of our not having enough chronological dots on the canvas to produce a consistent, consecutive, means of measurement throughout the two decades during which he was actively writing. But even if we did, the deliberately formal basis of the poems—different kinds of stanzas for each kind of poem—does not permit an overview of the different possibilities for experimentation in the same way that assessing the gradations and changes in the handling of blank verse allows. The most we can say about Shakespeare's evolution as a writer of poems is that his habits with verse forms took root in the 1590s, a highly charged decade for poetry as it was for drama. He wrote in some of the preferred genres of the day, as we will see, and was indifferent to others—the rise of verse satire, for instance. He explored and exhibited the period's great attraction to verbal ornamentation, rhetorical colouring, and copiousness of expression. He reduced their effects in the deliberately stringent 'The Phoenix and Turtle', in 1601, perhaps responding to the new trend for 'strong lines' and paradoxes favoured by the younger generation of Donne and Jonson. And he amplified them again in *A Lover's Complaint*, if we consider the work entirely his, when he was perhaps playing on a sense of nostalgia for things Elizabethan. But his continual or intermittent work on the Sonnets until their publication in 1609 does not reveal either a desire to keep up with the age, as his contemporary Michael Drayton tried to do, or the revisionary instincts of a modern poet like Yeats, constantly in search of more truthful forms of expression.

A commercial playwright had to keep up with what was trending, as we would say today, if he hoped to be successful. A poet didn't, at least not to the same degree. Indeed, in Shakespeare's day, plays were generally assumed to be ephemera. They were to involve two hours or so of traffic on the stage and then to be forgotten, or at least assigned to lesser venues for quick publication in the stalls around St Paul's Cathedral, as in the case of the quarto versions of the plays that were becoming one of the staples of a growing publishing industry that paralleled the growth of the theatre in the 1590s. Poetry's nobler pedigree included, rather, the aspiration to permanence, both in sentiment and practice, in manuscript form and through the printed medium of the book. It also included appealing to an elite audience of educated readers rather than to a more popular audience that frequented the great amphitheatres in Shakespeare's day, and the presence of 'The Phoenix and Turtle' in mid-career as part of a printed volume of patronage poems suggests Shakespeare's continuing taste for caviar amid the daily fare of playwriting.

In this scenario, writing for the stage was socially problematic, déclassé, mostly practised by the newly arrived in town (Shakespeare was from Stratford), sometimes possessing little education (only grammar school in his case), and their works—or more specifically their writings, which were owned by the companies, not by the authors—were often performed on the other side of the tracks. The tracks, in this case, was the Thames river: London's Southbank, home of bear-baiting and brothels alike—worse than Hollywood, or off-off Broadway, and certainly not London's fashionable West End. Writing poetry, on the other hand, at least certain kinds of poetry, was within the purview of aristocrats, even the reach of royalty. Both Queen Elizabeth and King James wrote verse. (The form in which Shakespeare wrote *Lucrece*, rhyme royal, in fact, is now named after the 15th-century King James I of Scotland.) So did many aspiring courtiers, like Sidney and Donne, even if they adhered to their sense of privilege by not letting their works be published.

Shakespeare worked both sides of town with considerable success, and, in doing so, participated, and imagined participating, in both versions of authorship. Hence his sometimes hyphenated status in scholarly circles as a 'Poet-Playwright', or to ramp up the significant place his work was coming to assume in his own lifetime and thereafter, 'National Poet-Playwright'. Shakespeare wrote poems to connect with the elite and the financial rewards that might come from patronage. He wrote drama to survive. That Shakespeare thrived financially in the theatre shouldn't prevent us from recognizing his desire to be perceived as a 'gentleman'. He not only purchased the second largest house in Stratford; he was also probably the person responsible for successfully renewing his father's request for a coat of arms in 1596. But as we know, too, his double occupation sometimes caused him pain and embarrassment. Nowhere is this self-contempt for his public life in the theatre expressed more vividly than in the famous 'dyer's hand' Sonnet (111), which begins, ruefully and apologetically, to his lover,

O, for my sake do you with Fortune chide,
The guilty goddess of my harmful deeds,
That did not better for my life provide
Than public means which public manners breeds.
Thence comes it that my name receives a brand,
And almost thence my nature is subdued
To what it works in, like the dyer's hand.

Here, Shakespeare blames his bad behaviour in love on his position in life, the self-indictment sounding particularly sharp in the double use of 'public' as an explanation that equates his 'means' with his 'manners'. To this anxious self-portrait, we might recall that Shakespeare's father was a glove-maker, and dyeing leather part of the job, a fact that brings the personal sense of stain in the poem closer yet to home. The sonnet exposes the uncomfortable gap which Shakespeare had to cross between public and private life, and between the elite and common worlds of the stratified England of the late 16th century. Such evident embarrassment might help to explain why he was slow to bring these poems into the daylight of print.

Stage and page: a sample comparison

Sociological explanations help us to understand the circumstances of Shakespeare as person and author, but there are other laws at work that illuminate fundamental differences between the two literary forms that were the mainstays of his livelihood, stage and page. Take as a case in point, a scene from *The Two Gentlemen of Verona* as it is re-worked in one of Shakespeare's sonnets. At the end of Act I, Proteus laments having to leave his home in Verona, where Julia resides, a situation that he has unwittingly and ironically created by lying to his father about the letter in his hand. He claims, falsely, that it is from his friend, Valentine, now in Milan, rather than from Julia, who will soon prove to be as steadfast in her love for Proteus as he will be fickle—or protean—in his love for her:

> Thus have I shunned the fire for fear of burning
> And drenched me in the sea where I am drowned.
> I feared to show my father Julia's letter
> Lest he should take exceptions to my love;
> And with the vantage of mine own excuse
> Hath he excepted most against my love.
> O, how this spring of love resembleth
> The uncertain glory of an April day,
> Which now shows all the beauty of the sun
> And by and by a cloud takes all away. (1.3.78–87)

The speech is a good example of Shakespeare's early style in the theatre—the sense of each line comporting almost exactly with its length—but its main purpose is to move the action along: to summarize briefly what has happened and to prepare for the transition to the next scene. Proteus concludes with a brief exclamation equating love's transience with 'The uncertain glory of an April day', a commonplace barely begun before being cut off by the entrance of his servant, Panthino: 'Sir Proteus your father calls for you. / He is in haste; therefore I pray you go'. The exigencies of plot are everything. Stage time rules. Shakespeare will quickly learn to manage the levers of scene change more smoothly, but the plays will always be driven by their own temporal circumstances.

A few years later, although exactly how many is uncertain, Shakespeare re-imagined such a moment in the following poem, observing a different set of rules. Three alternate rhyming quatrains, followed by a couplet, compose the standard sonnet form from which Shakespeare almost never varied and which now has acquired his name in order to differentiate it from the Petrarchan sonnet, which employs a different rhyme pattern:

Full many a glorious morning have I seen
Flatter the mountain tops with sovereign eye,
Kissing with golden face the meadows green,
Gilding pale streams with heavenly alchemy,
Anon permit the basest clouds to ride
With ugly rack on his celestial face,
And from the forlorn world his visage hide,
Stealing unseen to west with this disgrace:
Even so my sun one early morn did shine
With all triumphant splendor on my brow;
But out alack, he was but one hour mine,
The region cloud hath masked him from me now.
Yet him for this my love no whit disdaineth:
Suns of the world may stain, when heaven's sun staineth.

The scene is reminiscent of the situation in *The Two Gentlemen of Verona*, in which the springtime of love metaphorically resembles the uncertain glories of the day, but the fourteen lines of Sonnet 33 allow Shakespeare the opportunity to draw out the sweet and sour of love contained in this moment of departure. (*Romeo and Juliet* will soon make much of this experience on stage, which is one reason why that play seems so fully steeped in the sonnet tradition.) It's as if, metaphorically speaking, Shakespeare has exchanged a draughtsman's quill for a painter's brush. Against Proteus's brisk treatment of the same topic, we're now given amplitude of address and gradation of feelings, the nuances of reflection—thought coloured by emotion, beginning with a deep or 'full' inhale and then presented in something like slow motion as we move through the individual frames constituting the poem's structure. The reader will find personal licence for this kind of slow reading in verse in the famous scene in *Lucrece* depicting the fall of Troy, in which Lucrece lingers long and thoughtfully over specific details in the work. Here, in the sonnet, we pause over the artist's individual brush strokes, the lush use, for instance, of alliteration, a poet's stock-in-trade. 'Glorious', 'golden', 'green', and 'gilding' produce a glittering coronal of sound to accompany the regal or sovereign authority of the celestial sun, adding a sonic and emotional sway begun with the first word 'Full' and carried on in 'Flatter', and then further amplified in the pattern of active participial verbs initiating each line ('Kissing', 'Gilding').

But even more to the point we are struck, and have time to be struck, by the emotional drama of the love situation through the gathering force of the analogy. It is not until the turn in line 9 (often referred to as the 'volta'), with its reference to 'Even so', that we glimpse the true subject, the target of the simile, a simile made complex because of the sharp contrast drawn in the second quatrain in the sudden depiction ('anon') of the 'basest clouds' on the horizon. But the clouds don't just appear. They 'ride', and not just ride through the sky but 'ride with ugly rack on his celestial face', as if with a deliberate sense of delivering an insult. That word 'rack', moreover, not only carries with it the abstract sense of 'wreck', as in ruin, but perhaps, in conjunction with 'ugly', a tertiary suggestion of the instrument of pain itself: the rack commonly used to torture prisoners in Shakespeare's day. For Proteus in *The Two Gentlemen of Verona*, the cloud simply takes away the beauty of the Sun, 'by and by'. It's time for him to move on. In the Sonnet, beauty is first made magnificent, only to be redrawn as ugly, where the celestial face is then remade into an image ('a visage') of disgrace, of shame.

In this sonnet, where the speaker first discovers a flaw in his lover, the climax for the reader occurs when the speaker applies the octave's imagery to his personal experience: '*my* sun/*my* brow' (my italics). The shift represents a twist in the poem's argument but one that also carries through the complex of meanings established in the first two quatrains to shed a shadowy light on the lovers' relationship as felt by the speaker. Not simply is the temporality of affection described—he was but 'one hour mine'—and the matter of gender underscored, but now the suggestion of the lover's questionable motives intrude. Did he go out with someone else, or fail to return a phone call, as the

American poet Allen Ginsberg speculates, courting the anachronism? The distance measured between speaker and lover is not simply temporal or even spatial but moral, ethical, and personal, even epistemological, through the reference to the clouds having 'masked him from me *now*' (my italics). And does 'now' mean only for the moment? The concluding couplet, with its evident rationalization now masquerading as an explanation, suggests longer, indeed perhaps even permanently, in the manner of a 'stain', the poem's final troubling word.

Needless to say, this is not the kind of reading available in the theatre. But on the page it is. As with most of the Sonnets and Shakespeare's poetry more generally, Sonnet 33 invites close reading, not, however, because the author was engaged in a game of subtle circumlocution forced upon him by circumstances, or not only because of that possibility, but because he understood and was able to exploit the innuendos of language, its wanton duplicities and multiplicities, more fully than any other poet in the English language, especially in the field of love; because he believed that complexity of meaning and depth of feeling are congruent with, not opposed to, each other. It is certainly true that a contemporary reader of Shakespeare might have emphasized different features of the reading experience. That person, most often but not always male, would probably have been more drawn to the poem's proverbial sentiments, rhetorical coloration, and sophisticated grammatical patterns, reading habits deeply ingrained by educational and cultural attitudes of the time. But as important as it is to value these earlier practices, there is no reason to be bound by them any more than, when we attend the theatre, we should insist that all performances be measured by the attempt to replicate period dress and staging.

Some surprises

A few surprises persist in the reception history of Shakespeare's works that are worth noting. First, no one would have been more astonished by posterity's elevation of the plays over the poems than the author himself. This is not simply because the great folio publication of his plays, a publication that brought to light eighteen plays that would have been lost to sight forever, didn't happen until 1623, some seven years after his death in 1616. But during his lifetime, his fame as a poet, in some quarters, clearly exceeded his growing reputation as a successful playwright. If one considers the medium of print only as an index of popularity, *Venus and Adonis* far outstripped any of the plays in number of editions, going through ten editions by 1617 and another six by 1640 (to say nothing about its further circulation in manuscript format and commonplace books of the period). By comparison *Richard III*, the most frequently re-printed of the plays, went through only six editions by 1622, the year preceding the publication of the First Folio. The figures are only slightly less impressive for *Lucrece*, but together, in the period from 1593 to 1623, the narrative poems constituted an astonishing 40 per cent of all Shakespeare's published works.

A second surprise, of the opposite kind, is that the *Sonnets*, the book of poems that has seemed among the best loved in the English language and a cornerstone of the educational system in English for well over a century, was received in its day in almost complete silence. Few great books have left, initially, so small a trail. Indeed, almost from the start, the *Sonnets* and the narrative poems have been on opposite sides of the playing field, with the initially disregarded *Sonnets* only surpassing in popularity the narrative poems in the early 19th century when the Romantic ideal of the lyric in general and the penchant for autobiography in particular pushed the *Sonnets* into full (and sometimes troubling) view, even ahead of the plays in some quarters. The clear preference for the *Sonnets* over the narrative poems remained largely in place throughout the 20th century, in part because, in professional circles, the practices of New Criticism at mid-century were better honed for analysing and teaching short lyrics than longer narratives. But while the general popularity of the *Sonnets* continues on a variety of fronts—they can be read on the subway or in the classroom or in yet more private spaces—the advent of other modes of criticism, especially those inspired by feminists in the early 1970s, has returned the narrative poems, with their remarkable females, to a level of popularity among readers that they haven't enjoyed since the early 17th century.

Later chapters will develop many of the points made in this introductory chapter, but one summary observation remains to be made. Tastes change and so do modes of mediation and habits of reading. Few writers and their works can match the permutations that Shakespeare's works have undergone and continue to undergo. In his own lifetime, the occasionally acted play of his was turned into print in ways that measure his growing status as an author, as a poet-playwright. Drama, as a separate form, was then expanded through Folio publication—four alone in the 17th century—where it became a *body* of work for posterity to study, analyse, and perform. And much later film, repeatedly, circulated the plays to a wider audience beyond the theatre, and the internet now wider still, to almost anywhere on the planet.

The poems have not been ignored in this process, although the story of their afterlife in this *Short Introduction* will be limited to the Anglophone world. The Sonnets have a long history of being spoken aloud, sung, turned into art songs, their passions even acted out or danced on stage, and the same has been true for the narrative poems, which, of late, have shown themselves to be especially receptive to multi-media presentations. The internet, too, is crowded with Shakespearean verse—not all of which is authored by Shakespeare, it needs to be said. But while it is often thought and frequently remarked that the fullest realization of the plays is through their performance on stage, the same cannot be said of the poems. They were not written as scripts for pageants. Their natural home is on the page, their life brought into being by the individual reader, wherever memory retains or a serviceable text is within reach. Although sometimes nearly lost to sight in

15

massive modern editions of Shakespeare's Works, it is part of the story of their continuing rise to prominence that so many excellent editions now exist of the poems. And one of the best, by Colin Burrow, is now dedicated to what never happened in Shakespeare's lifetime and rarely ever satisfactorily since: an edition of *The Complete Sonnets and Poems*.

Chapter 2
Venus and Adonis

Sexy subject, attractive layout

Venus and Adonis—Shakespeare's best-selling first venture into print, a poem soon to become one of the era's most popular works—is a young person's poem, written by a 29-year-old emerging poet, about the topsy-turvy, innocent yet dangerous impulses of sexual desire. Although often comical, Venus's hot pursuit of the young Adonis ends in his being gored by a boar. The near rhyme is almost a pun, as proximate and painfully inevitable as the familiar equation in the period between sex and death.

Along with showing off the young Shakespeare's budding genius, three separate ingredients served as immediate catalysts for the poem: an outbreak of the plague, the re-invention of an erotic literary form, and an irascible comment by a contemporary. In 1593, the year the poem was published, the plague was raging through London and, as required by law, the theatres were closed in response. The disease claimed the lives of approximately 10,000 Londoners that year, out of a general population of about 200,000. Although the poem is hardly topical, the disease, like love itself, left its deadly mark. As with poets of the recent past addressing the AIDS epidemic, here is the narrator thinking wishfully about so much, including that his hero and heroine's youthful passion, their vitality ('verdour'), would have a curative effect:

> Long may they kiss each other for this cure.
> O never let their crimson liveries [lips] wear,
> And as they last, their verdour still endure,
> To drive infection from the dangerous year,
>> That the star-gazers [astrologers], having writ on death,
>> May say the plague is banished by thy breath. (ll. 505–10)

The death/breath rhyme cinches a fantasy, but touchingly so.

Needing to survive—and, one assumes, to help support his family back in Stratford—Shakespeare sought to exploit another kind of writing besides drama: the *epyllion*. The little epic, or, as it has also come to be known, the erotic narrative poem, derived inspiration from Ovid's writings, particularly his vastly popular *Metamorphoses*, which had been translated into English by the prolific Arthur Golding in 1567. This largely Elizabethan enthusiasm for the epyllion was of recent invention in England. It dated back to a rather innocuous poem in 1589 by Thomas Lodge called *Scylla's Metamorphosis*. The quickly developing vogue was largely aimed at the idle but rambunctious sort of male readers down from Oxford or Cambridge, or studying at one of the Inns of Court in London (none of which Shakespeare attended)—just the kind of person, in fact, Shakespeare would poke fun at a few years later in the figure of the elderly Justice Shallow in *2 Henry 4*, 'lusty Shallow', reminiscing rather fantastically about his youth spent at Clement's Inn chasing after the 'bona-robas'.

This minor epic mode was also soon to enlist the likes of Thomas Nash and Christopher Marlowe, among others. Nash was quick to produce a raunchy bit of smut called *A Choice of Valentines* (1593) and Marlowe the far more artful *Hero and Leander* (1593), the only poem of comparable literary merit to *Venus and Adonis*. After several other flares by Thomas Heywood and Michael Drayton, the flame died down. But in its early, brightest phase, the Ovidian erotic poem helped to launch Shakespeare's career as a poet—and John Donne's as well, although Donne wasn't looking for a literary career, born into aristocratic circumstances as he was and largely eschewing the vulgar world of print in favour of the more elite readership associated with manuscript circulation.

But the Stratfordian Shakespeare was, by necessity. And here's the last—or at least another—ingredient that went into the poem's making. In part because of his lack of academic and social pedigree, Shakespeare had been labelled an 'upstart crow' in a satirical pamphlet called *Greene's Groatsworth of Wit* (1592). Robert Greene was a Cambridge graduate and a cranky and prolific writer, although perhaps not the author of this pamphlet, which is sometimes assigned to Henry Chettle. In any case, the insult, followed by a riff on a line from Shakespeare's *Titus Andronicus*, was an example of the competitive mud-slinging that marked Shakespeare's early days in the theatre as the acting companies, the playwrights, and their patrons attempted to sort things out. It's hard for modern readers to think back on a time when Shakespeare wasn't Olympian—like Prospero calling on all those 'cloud capped towers' in *The Tempest*. But early on he needed to make his way, to become prosperous. *Venus and Adonis* was an alluring avenue to pursue when others were blocked, and Shakespeare used it, rather pointedly and perhaps anxiously, to elevate himself above lowly groundlings and fellow rival dramatists and poets, including perhaps the recently deceased Marlowe of *Hero and Leander*.

For the first and only time in his career, Shakespeare publicly asserted his Apollonian status as a poet. An epigraph in Latin from Ovid's *Amores* appears on the poem's highly crafted title page: *Vilia miretur vulgus: mihi flavus Apollo/Pocula Castalia plena ministret aqua* ('Let the common herd be amazed by worthless things; but for me let golden Apollo provide cups full of the water of the Muses') (Figure 1). And for the first but not the only time, he sought a patron for his poem: 'the Right Honourable

19

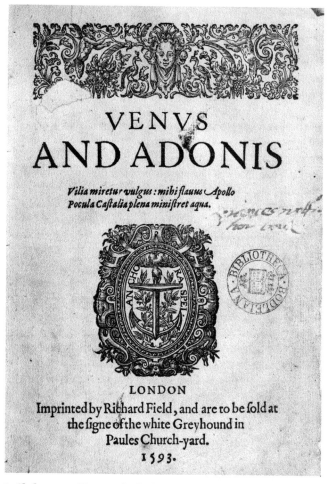

VENVS
AND ADONIS

Vilia miretur vulgus : mihi flauus Apollo
Pocula Castalia plena ministret aqua.

LONDON

Imprinted by Richard Field, and are to be sold at
the signe of the white Greyhound in
Paules Church-yard.
1593.

1. Shakespeare, *Venus and Adonis*, 1593. Title page.

Henry Wriothesley, Earl of Southampton, and Baron of Titchfield',
as the title page to the Dedication declares. The dedicatory page
also bore the name 'William Shakespeare'. It was the first time for
this as well.

Wriothesley (pronounced 'Risley') is a fascinating figure. Ten years younger than Shakespeare, the handsome, impetuous, apparently wealthy, 19-year-old earl was much sought after as a patron by poets in the early 1590s, although it appears he didn't have much money until later, when he came into his estate in 1596 (Figure 2). How the two men came into contact is a matter of conjecture,

2. Portrait of Henry Wriothesley, 3rd Earl of Southampton.

as is the extent and depth of their friendship. *Lucrece* would bear a warmer dedication to Wriothesley, but after that the trail goes cold, and uncertainties, but not impossibilities, abound. Wriothesley is perhaps alluded to in Sonnet 107, and he has been frequently and sometimes ingeniously identified as the 'fair youth' of Shakespeare's Sonnets as well as the mysterious dedicatee, 'the onlie begetter', of the volume. There are other potential connections as well, but for present purposes, it is perhaps enough that his feminine good looks and physical grace might liken him, up to a point, to a young Adonis. The stir he seems to have caused among the writers has its erotic parallel in Venus's specific reactions to 'Rose-cheeked Adonis' and in the poem's sexually charged field more generally.

The closing of the theatres, in effect, opened a different set of doors. This one admitted a more select audience who might see a lowly dramatist, a mountebank who trafficked in shows and shadows (and who was himself a shadow, an actor), in a more exalted light: as a poet of fine craftsmanship, working in a familiar form, on a subject of minor but unusual classical interest. In a move that smacks more of the print-conscious Jonson, Shakespeare also teamed up with the printer Richard Field. Field was from Stratford, too, and had already published some notable books, including literary works such as George Puttenham's *Art of English Poesy* (1589) and Ovid's *Metamorphoses* (1589). Although Shakespeare's publishing connection with Field was to be short-lived, he nonetheless emerged in print with a well-designed book: a sophisticated cover and an attractive page layout of Roman typeface, rather than the usual run-of-the-mill blackletter gothic associated with the popular or ephemeral literature of the day, including Lodge's *Scylla's Metamorphosis*. *Venus and Adonis* was made, in short, to be a good read, especially for an appreciative upscale audience. Capturing the contemporary buzz swirling around the poem, Spenser's friend, Gabriel Harvey, wrote a few years later in a note in his 1598 copy of Chaucer: 'the younger sort takes much delight in Shakespeares Venus, & Adonis', and then continued in a more elderly vein, 'but his Lucrece, & his tragedie of Hamlet, Prince of Denmarke, have it in them, to please the wiser sort'.

Erotic Venus

Shakespeare's poem has since become attractive reading material for people of varying ages and differing sexes. This trend began early on in the 17th century when, among other titillating responses, the poem incited male readers to fantasize about females reading the book in private. It continues today in the different kinds of criticism the poem has provoked from both male and female critics, straight and gay, ranging across a wide field of interpretation. These include allegory, stylistics, psychoanalysis, feminism, and queer theory—to say nothing about the autobiographical possibilities underlying a tale in which an older woman pursues a younger man. (Shakespeare was seven years younger than his wife, Anne Hathaway.) Whatever the approach, the expanded readership of *Venus and Adonis* is due in large part to the complex characterization of Venus herself. She is given the lion's share of the lines: 592 compared to Adonis's scant eighty-seven.

Venus is more than a prototype of a porn star or the luxuriously erotic model in a Renaissance painting by Titian or Velasquez, although she certainly has features of each. 'I hate not love, but your device in love,' complains an overwhelmed Adonis, 'That lends embracements unto every stranger' (ll. 789–90). The most famous passage in the poem is what has come to be known as 'the deer park' simile. It invites the reader (or more specifically Adonis) to imagine Venus in full reclining posture, a diva who is also nature's divan:

> 'Fondling,' she saith, 'Since I have hemmed thee here
> Within the circuit of this ivory pale,
> I'll be a park, and thou shalt be my deer:

Feed where thou wilt, on mountain, or in dale;
　　Graze on my lips, and if those hills be dry,
　　Stray lower, where the pleasant fountains lie.

Within this limit is relief enough,
Sweet bottom grass, and high delightful plain,
Round rising hillocks, brakes obscure and rough,
To shelter thee from tempest, and from rain:
　　Then be my deer, since I am such a park.
　　No dog shall rouse thee, though a thousand bark.' (ll. 229–40)

It's easy to see why this passage immediately caught fire. (In less than a year, it was already being mimicked by Thomas Heywood: 'Be Phaoe's boatman, I will be thy barke.') The passage is exuberantly written—the scene sharply realized, euphemistically witty, and yet it leaves room for the fancy to roam. One can readily imagine any number of Hollywood stars aching for lines like these to deliver. It's also funny and a bit weird. Sophisticates might be used to seeing a lap-dog in erotic paintings of the period (as in Titian's so-called 'Venus of Urbino', now in the Uffizi Gallery in Florence), but a deer, the object of desire and hallmark of Petrarchan poetry through the pun on 'dear'? And more often than not in the erotic poetry of the period, while we're familiar with the male poet likening the female body to nature, it is surprising, even shocking, to discover that the person speaking so boldly is a woman. You can do things with thoughts on the page that cannot be acted out on the stage.

There is something auto-erotic and therefore self-empowering in Venus's description, yet as spoken to an indifferent Adonis, it is also tinged with an element of desperation that the poem will amplify. Venus's sexual fantasy can appeal to male and female readers alike, and keep appealing because it is never consummated in the text, although perhaps not to a male worried about being hemmed in and emasculated, or uninterested in the opposite sex, both of which are active possibilities with Shakespeare's rather icy Adonis. But even here one must be careful about over-generalizing the varied responses this poem has ignited. Desire is loopy in *Venus and Adonis*. Observes John Addington Symonds, the Victorian scholar of the Italian Renaissance, a poet, and early writer on same-sex male love, Venus's 'hot wooing taught me what it was to woo with sexual ardour. I dreamed of falling back like her upon the grass, and folding the quick-panting lad in my embrace.'

An odd couple: revising Ovid

The 'deer park' passage cuts in many unexpected directions, as does the poem, whose variety of Venusian subject matter owes something to the encyclopedic habits of popular Renaissance mythologists like Natale Conti. (Conti has a chapter each on Venus and Adonis in his *Mythologiae*, initially published in 1567 and many times thereafter.) Shakespeare's specific debt, though, is to Ovid's *Metamorphoses*, Book 10, the interpolated tale of Venus and Adonis as voiced by Orpheus, the one-time lover of Eurydice who later became a lover of young boys. In Ovid's version, the goddess, charmed by Adonis's youthful beauty, falls passionately in love with the young man. Shakespeare's reworking of the episode would seem less striking, that is, more familiar, if he had stuck to Ovid's story in one important respect: casting Venus and Adonis as lovers—the beautiful young man and the love-struck goddess, who do enjoy a night together before Adonis goes off to hunt the boar, against Venus's strong warnings, and is killed.

This is the version that Titian presumably had in mind in his sensuous rendering of the parting scene between the two in his famous painting originally executed for Philip II of Spain—a visual analogue and cultural resource for how early modern people thought about the couple (Figure 3). In the painting, Adonis is youthful and masculine, Venus voluptuous and feminine. But not so in Shakespeare: the poet made Venus not only a passionately aggressive female playing many roles traditionally assigned to the male wooer (as in the 'deer park' simile); he made the boyish

25

3. Titian, *Venus and Adonis*, c.1555–60.

'Rose-cheeked Adonis' a steadfast disdainer of her offerings.
Along with admitting possible homoerotic responses to the poem
(witness Symonds' reaction) that accompanied the period interest
in Ovidian tales, Shakespeare laid the groundwork for essentially
a dramatic, and at times melodramatic, treatment of his subject,
even perhaps operatic, if we regard Henry Purcell's *Dido* as a
descendant of this constellation of abandoned classical women
revived in the Renaissance.

In Shakespeare's poem, in which power and desire are at
loggerheads, one character serves as foil to the other. A sexually,
verbally capacious goddess is set against an emotionally
undeveloped, tight-lipped human. But the two also don't hold
the imaginary stage alone. There is a third figure, or character
(just as there is a boar to fill out love's triangle in this complex
account of desire): the narrator or speaker, who frames and

frequently interprets the story through brief asides, similes, extended metaphors, exclamations, sophisticated comparisons, and elaborate conceits, as in the case of the notorious, baroque, 'shelly cave' simile quickly lampooned by contemporaries (ll. 1032–48). In these multiple activities, he is much more present than the narrator in Ovid. Shakespeare's narrator seems, as it were, to occupy a front row seat in a story of his own telling.

Art and poetry

Braided together, the whole yields a deftly woven tapestry—to borrow a term for poetry that had special currency in Shakespeare's day thanks to Sir Philip Sidney's *Defense of Poetry*, in which it is boldly claimed that all of nature's abundance cannot equal what poetry can reproduce. (In Book Three of *The Faerie Queene*, 'The Legend of Chastity', Spenser, in fact, represents the tale of Venus and Adonis as woven on a tapestry in Castle Joyous.) And as tapestries frequently made amatory and hunting scenes their subjects, thus linking wooing and predation, the same may be said for the refracted story of *Venus and Adonis*. Venus hunts Adonis, while Adonis chases after the boar in an English-seeming landscape rich with flora and fauna, roses and rabbits, although not depicted in the beautifully carpeted, lushly descriptive manner of Marlowe's *Hero and Leander*.

Shakespeare's poem is more angular and abrupt, composed largely of set speeches, many on familiar topics of the day involving love and loss, wooing and mourning. The familiarity surely accounts for some of the poem's immediate appeal, while the sharp turns of thought and plot keep offering surprises. (The famously startling stage direction in *The Winter's Tale*, 'exit pursued by bear', might be seen in embryo in the sudden appearance of 'a breeding jennet' rushing forth to mate with Adonis's horse in line 260.) Delivered mostly by Venus over the course of her two days and a night with Adonis, the speeches leading up to his departure generally focus on her ravenous desire for at least a kiss, somewhat desperately received by him as the sun goes down (ll. 535–45), and they contain some odd twists and sudden digressions of an often exemplary kind borrowed from the natural environment—all delivered using a six-line verse stanza, of which more must be said.

Often called a 'sixain' in Shakespeare's day, the stanza was recognized by contemporaries as 'not only most usual, but also very pleasant to the ear'. In Shakespeare's hands, the form enabled variety and precision, room for amplification in its alternating rhymes in the quatrain, and concision in its closing couplet, the two together completing an ear-pleasing arc of thought as the rhetorician George Puttenham wished. Here is Venus starting her campaign:

> 'Thrice fairer than myself,' thus she began,
> 'The field's chief flower, sweet above compare,
> Stain to all nymphs, more lovely than a man,
> More white and red than doves or roses are:
> > Nature that made thee with herself at strife,
> > Saith that the world hath ending with thy life.' (ll. 7–12)

You can feel Shakespeare's immediate confidence with the form, as if the son of a glove-maker were slipping on a perfectly fitted item, with all the creases in the right place, rather than, as was the case, trying it on for the first time. *Venus and Adonis* was woven out of 199 such stanzas. By the late 19th century, the well-worn glove itself would be called 'the Venus and Adonis' stanza, an instance of Shakespeare's fame at work.

A youthful poem, *Venus and Adonis* owes much to humanist training in rhetoric. As literary scholars have often remarked, Venus is associated with Renaissance stylistic ideas of *copia* or abundance. Her natural rhetorical mode is expansion by comparison, with herself typically serving as the starting point, a practice that quickly develops in this stanza into other areas of beauty's consideration ('more lovely', 'more white and red'). Indeed, more than anyone, Venus is responsible for the poem's fast-paced energy, often brought to a sharp point, as in the above, with a tight couplet and strong rhyme, a sense of verbal movement mirrored in her bodily power as she takes charge of the action in her attempt to satisfy her desire. She will shortly be seen plucking Adonis from his horse, and, virago-like, taking control of both horse and rider: 'Over one arm the lusty courser's rein, / Under her other was the tender boy' (ll. 31–2). And the narrator will parenthetically but enthusiastically exclaim from the sideline: 'O how quick is love!' (l. 38). 'Quick' immediately associates Venus, not Adonis, with vigour and energy, as if she were striding across a stage. She is a force of life, up to a point.

We can also see in this passage a measure of Shakespeare's skill at weaving together what will be the poem's larger story. He introduces images or phrases that will grow in meaning, not just in Venus's identification with nature, but in her association of Adonis with the 'field's chief flower'. The image points at once to his exceptional beauty and his frailty, and anticipates his later transformation into 'a purple flower ... chequered with white' (l. 1168). So, too, 'stain' will be redirected from what Adonis is reported, figuratively, to do 'to all nymphs' to what is actually done to him by the boar and which Venus will do to herself; and his beauty, 'more lovely than a man', will hint at the later fatal effects of his attractiveness when he is gored in the thigh by the boar's tusk. With the benefit of hindsight, we can see, in the closing couplet rhyming 'strife' and 'life', a hint of Venus's extended grief over the death of Adonis, her lengthy, moving lament (ll. 1075–1120), which will end not in the world's end, but with her walling herself off from the world by returning to Paphos, the city in Cyprus sacred to her. For all its rapidity of movement, the poem sustains—and rewards—careful reading.

If Shakespeare associates Venus throughout with various elements of 'quickness', he identifies Adonis with its near elemental opposite, coolness. Adonis's usual mode of speech is that of curt utterance. For all Venus's pleading, his heart remains largely unstirred, unmoved, 'to temptation slow', in the words of Sonnet 94, leaving the narrator at one point early on to comment on the essential impossibility, or absurdity, of their pairing: 'Backward she pushed him, as she would be thrust, / And governed him in strength though not in lust' (ll. 41–2). A great rhyming clinch (feel the masculine force in the wishful phrase 'as she would be thrust'), but there's nothing, or almost nothing, Venus can do to will her end, not even, as this passage comes close to suggesting, if she tried to rape Adonis. Comical as it might seem—the poem has farcical moments reminiscent of Shakespeare's early play, *The Comedy of Errors*—the couplet cannot make a couple out of them.

What the stark opposition and situations between her will and Adonis's do furnish, however, is verbal opportunity for Venus. Her rhetorical performances act as a form of sublimation for the thing she cannot get, which both amplify the subject of desire and show off the poet's wares in the hopes of amplifying his literary prospects. Indeed, Venus's dilemma, her paradoxical situation, is adroitly suggested by the narrator in a single, compact line that makes an epigrammatic feat (and feast) out of desire itself: 'She's love, she loves, and yet she is not loved' (l. 610). Shakespeare is indulging here in a small rhetorical flourish called *polyptoton*, in this case the triple redeployment of a single word (love) in three different grammatical senses: as proper noun, as present-tense verb, and as past participle of a verb. Remember 'love' in its multiplying reflections, the line seems to say, and the line has not been forgotten by many since.

In a similar manner, through Venus (sometimes in conjunction with the narrator), Shakespeare can expand his poem by expounding a few familiar Renaissance *topoi* or commonplace

ideas, made only slightly strange as voiced by a female.
His Venus can play ardent lover in *carpe diem* fashion: 'Fair
flowers that are not gathered in their prime / Rot, and consume
themselves in little time' (ll. 131–2). She can brandish her
credentials as a lover even of Mars, the god of war: 'Over my
altars hath he hung his lance' (l. 103). She can argue for sex
on the basis of the need for fruition (ll. 169–70), or as a banquet
of sense, delightful in itself (ll. 427–50); criticize Adonis on the
grounds of his being narcissistic (l. 161); insult him on the
basis of his family history and incestuous genealogy (ll. 211–16);
and use the natural activities of horses to instruct him in his
masculine obligations.

These are speeches that might well appeal to a gentrified readership
not just knowingly literate but interested in genealogy as well as
horsemanship, and possessing at least a smattering of knowledge
about the arts, as England struggled to catch up with the continent
in this regard:

> 'Fie, lifeless picture, cold, and senseless stone,
> Well-painted idol, image dull, and dead,
> Statue contenting but the eye alone,
> Thing like a man, but of no woman bred:
> Thou art no man, though of a man's complexion,
> For men will kiss even by their own direction.' (ll. 211–16)

Venus can cast insults with the best of Shakespeare's stage
characters. Her hit on Adonis's masculinity is to the point, if
hardly subtle: 'Thing like a man' reduces him on the spot,
carrying the secondary, emasculating sense of his possessing a
'thing' (penis) in appearance only. The inter-art allusion to his
being a 'lifeless picture' goes in a different direction, deepened and
expanded in the reference to Adonis being a 'Statue contenting
but the eye alone'—and more interesting still for a reader who
already knows or is willing to study up on Adonis's unusual
lineage in *The Metamorphoses*.

Part of the fun of *Venus and Adonis* comes from the opportunity to explore the brilliantly generative source underlying it. In Ovid, Adonis descends from Pygmalion, the legendary sculptor from Cyprus, in a heady line of descent that originates with Pygmalion's falling in love with his own creation, a beautiful female statue. As the story goes, in answer to Pygmalion's prayers to Venus, the unnamed statue comes alive. From their union, however, also comes trouble. The two produce a daughter, Paphos. She in turn begets a son, Cinyras, who begets a daughter, Myrrha, who can't resist a passionate desire to sleep with Cinyras, her father. Adonis is the child of their incestuous union. He thus carries in his genes, so to speak, not only a legacy of cold narcissism (of the sculptor for his creation) but of sexual shame as well. Shakespeare has tidied up the back-story a bit. His reference to Adonis's being bred of 'no woman' glosses over the account in Ovid of Adonis's truly horrific birth. But knowledge of his genealogy, interesting in its own right, helps a reader understand why Shakespeare's Adonis might not want to have much to do with sex, let alone breeding, especially with Venus. His aversion to women is deep-seated, or deep-seeded.

Shakespeare will return to the story of Pygmalion near the end of his career when he integrates it, in surprising fashion, into the plot of *The Winter's Tale*. In *Venus and Adonis*, the reference to the sculpture is part of a trio of inter-art set-pieces. The most familiar is a reference to Pliny's famous account of the Greek painter Zeuxis, who depicted grapes so realistically that he deceived the eyes of the 'poor birds' themselves 'that helpless berries saw' (l. 604). The analogy serves as a metaphor for Venus's helpless situation of unfilled desire, and the poet's art at depicting her passion. The most elaborate allusion occurs in a lengthy digression on Adonis's sexually aroused horse (ll. 258–318). The main point of the digression is to offer Venus a teaching moment to instruct her recalcitrant student on the natural functions of breeding; but true to Ovid's interpolative methods of interlacing a tale within a tale, the account issues in a further digression on the rivalry between art and nature:

Look when a painter would surpass the life
In limning out a well-proportioned steed,
His art with nature's workmanship at strife,
As if the dead the living should exceed:
  So did this horse excel a common one
  In shape, in courage, colour, pace, and bone. (ll. 289–94)

And then, implicitly, a further competition: that between painting and poetry, in what is sometimes known as a *paragone*, after Leonardo's discussion of the rivalry between these two different forms of representation.

In the noun-laden blazon of the horse, beginning with the hoof, we can see Shakespeare marking out his poetic ground here in this first venture into print.

Round-hoofed, short-jointed, fetlocks shag and long,
Broad breast, full eye, small head, and nostril wide,
High crest, short ears, straight legs and passing strong,
Thin mane, thick tail, broad buttock, tender hide.
  Look what a horse should have he did not lack,
  Save a proud rider on so proud a back. (ll. 295–300)

One could make a drawing out of so precise a description, 'save' for the last line, which carries a meaning beyond what can be readily depicted and seen—the missing rider, Adonis. And missing for what reason we might wonder. Too young to take control of his passions, as represented by the horse? Too chiselled and cool to indulge them? Too prideful to stoop? Shakespeare's Adonis is something of a cipher, an absent rider.

Where do our sympathies lie?

In this poem of opposites and contrasts, we might readily ask with whom do our sympathies most reside? With Venus or Adonis? The answer is not as simple as it might first seem. Because Venus has the most lines—and is the rebuffed lover, who ultimately suffers the loss of her beloved—there is a temptation to read the poem largely from her point of view, especially when the narrator's sympathies encourage us in this direction. After a particularly heated moment in the poem, for instance, indeed after what might be called Venus's false climax in which she has delusions of sexual intercourse—'Now is she in the very lists of love' (l. 595)—we're quickly reminded by the narrator, 'But all in vain. Good queen, it will not be' (l. 607). It's the reference to her as 'Good queen' that keeps us on her side for the moment, as her wish for 'continual kissing' seems motivated by a desire to kindle 'the warm effects which she in him finds missing', as if resuscitating him.

Because Adonis is exceptionally tight-lipped, it is also difficult to read the poem strictly, or sympathetically, from his point of view. This distancing is a feature of his mode of utterance, not the limited number of lines he speaks. His biggest speech, in fact, given just before departing on the hunt, is a piece of textbook oratory, spoken by someone too young to know much about his subject.

> 'Love comforteth like sunshine after rain;
> But Lust's effect is tempest after sun;
> Love's gentle spring doth always fresh remain;
> Lust's winter comes ere summer half be done;
>   Love surfeits not; Lust like a glutton dies:
>   Love is all truth; Lust full of forgèd lies.
>
> More I could tell, but more I dare not say:
> The text is old, the orator too green.' (ll. 799–806)

And yet in this tweedle-dee, tweedle-dum version of love versus lust, Adonis is not quite as priggish or callow as this passage makes him seem: in part because he has some distance on himself (he is not so 'green' as to fail to take account of his greenness), and because, however old 'The text', it is not entirely without relevance to the situation on hand. What he says is, to a degree, to the point. Passion for Venus may be variable, but it is also relentless and ungovernable. It runs the gamut from self-less love to selfish lust; the 'warm effects' in the previous quotation are life-giving, but also potentially carnivorous. In fact, at the extreme, Adonis's association of lust and gluttony has been anticipated by the narrator through an extended comparison of Venus to a greedy vulture at the moment, no less, of their kissing (ll. 545–52), a simile that only grows in its capacity for incorporating violence. The same image will reappear in *The Rape of Lucrece*.

To put Adonis's plight in today's parlance, but with a twist: he is the abused, Venus the abuser. He is most sympathetic when pleading his need for space of his own:

> 'Fair Queen,' quoth he, 'If any love you owe me,
> Measure my strangeness with my unripe years.
> Before I know myself seek not to know me.
> No fisher but the ungrown fry forbears;
>> The mellow plum doth fall, the green sticks fast,
>> Or being early plucked is sour to taste.' (ll. 523–8)

The first three lines have immediate emotional appeal—the making of a part written for the stage, where the action might allow for some element of his growth. The different sense of 'know' is very much to the point in a poem where one meaning—his desire for self-knowledge—fends off against her desire to know him sexually. What prevents our sympathies from developing further, however, is not just reckoning the behaviour of his opposite number, Venus, but understanding the limited discourse the poem allots to Adonis. The subsequent three lines close the door on the prospect of further self-relation, on his development, with a series of proverbial utterances or proofs. At this point in the story, plot intervenes. There is nowhere for the reader to go with Adonis, just as Adonis has nowhere to go, or to grow, but to seek out the boar.

Separation anxieties

The dramatic moment of their separation is the subject of Titian's great painting—Venus's body restraining mightily to prevent Adonis from leaving, their legs going in opposite directions, but their faces turned toward each other, their eyes glued for one last time. In Shakespeare's version, there is no glue. Their separation is accomplished in two lines, with the emphasis on Adonis breaking free 'from the sweet embrace / Of those fair arms which bound him to her breast, / And homeward through the dark laund [glade] runs apace, / Leaves love upon her back, deeply distressed' (ll. 811–14). Venus is the abandoned lover, on her back once again, although no longer comically; but Shakespeare also rises to the occasion with some brilliant scene painting of his own, as Coleridge was the first critic to recognize:

> Look how a bright star shooteth from the sky;
> So glides he in the night from Venus' eye,
>
> Which after him she darts, as one on shore
> Gazing upon a late embarkèd friend,
> Till the wild waves will have him seen no more,
> Whose ridges with the meeting clouds contend:
> So did the merciless and pitchy night
> Fold in the object that did feed her sight. (ll. 815–22)

Writes one editor of the poem:

> This magical simile plays on *from*: it suggests that Venus is the point of Adonis's origin as the sky is the origin of the shooting star, and so presents the scene *from* her point of view; it also suggests with a simple objectivity that Adonis glides away *from* Venus's sight.

I have included the additional lines from the poem in order to complete the sense, unusual in requiring another stanza, as our eyes follow Venus's across the gap, only to participate in Adonis's disappearance from sight and the absolute 'merciless'—and yet also magnificent—finality of the second simile.

In Ovid, when Adonis leaves Venus, the tale is all but over. The goddess departs, Adonis is slain by the boar, and Venus pledges an annual ritual of mourning, begun by her sprinkling some sweet smelling nectar on his blood and his subsequent transformation into an anemone. (Spenser will remember and celebrate this annual rite in 'The Garden of Adonis' episode in *The Faerie Queene*.) Ten times longer than Ovid's compact ending, Shakespeare practically builds a whole other poem out of Adonis's loss but not in the direction that might appeal to Renaissance allegorists, who associated Venus with the Earth, Adonis with the Sun, and the Boar with winter. Venus, rather, is the solitary locus of consciousness in the latter part of Shakespeare's poem. She holds centre stage in much the same manner as Cleopatra does in the fifth act of *Antony and Cleopatra*, long after the death of Mark Antony, who, like the dead Adonis, grows in stature and in intimacy in Shakespeare's tragedy through the eulogizing process itself. Alone in the landscape, Shakespeare has Venus oscillating, nearly interminably it seems, between hope and despair with regard to Adonis's fate. She even acquires, in her movements, a physical vulnerability she did not earlier possess: 'And as she runs the bushes in the way / Some catch her by the neck, some kiss her face, / Some twined about her thighs to make her stay' (ll. 871-3). Not that she doesn't curse, as the convention of grieving often required. But in her case the curses are aimed at the personified figure of Death, a favourite Elizabethan target, and they include, in the form of prophecy, a pronouncement against 'all love's pleasures' (l. 1140). Her curses spring, that is, from an acutely registered sense of loss, not from personal venom further soured by dynastic spite, as in the case of the grieving mothers in, say, *Richard III*, written about the same time as *Venus and Adonis*, but as measured by her eyes and tears, and mingled with other emotions and effects. 'Variable passions throng her constant woe, / As striving who should best become her grief' (ll. 967-8). 'Alas,

poor world, what treasure hast thou lost, / What face remains
alive that's worth the viewing?' (ll. 1075–6).

Violence and the boar

Venus arrives at these distilled moments of grief—'Bonnet
nor veil henceforth no creature wear' (l. 1081)—only after her
twice-told encounter with the boar, the most memorable event in the
poem after the 'deer park' simile. Shakespeare has displaced the
wound Adonis suffered onto the witness, in what is one of his
earliest attempts at rendering the psychological processes associated
with extreme violence. Twice Venus sees the bloody boar, but only
the second time does she register the full impact, the significance,
of what has happened when she 'spies / The foul boar's conquest
on her fair delight. / Which seen, her eyes are murdered with the
view: / Like stars ashamed of day themselves withdrew' (ll. 1029–32).
A more mature Shakespeare will use the resources of theatrical
space and the mimetic capacity of distracted speech to represent
madness, especially in the cases of Ophelia, Lady Macbeth, Othello,
and Lear. Early in his dramatic career, he tends to objectify and
theatricalize violence through over-precise description, as in the case
of Marcus's detailing, in the manner of a blazon, the wounds that
Lavinia has suffered in *Titus Andronicus*.

Within the narrative terms of *Venus and Adonis*, Shakespeare is
indebted to the early practice of aestheticizing violence but also
inching toward the later psychotic representation. We understand
the traumatic effects of Adonis's death on Venus not through the
agency of distracted speech but through a narrative rupture that
features her distraught spectatorship. The 'shelly cave' simile,
for all its elaborate contortions, indeed because of its elaborate
contortions, describes the long moment of her traumatized psyche.
The whole process covers three stanzas as Venus seeks to escape
what the eyes have seen, a burden felt by the reader as well through
the piling on of clauses and similes describing upheavals in the
political and natural order. One can imagine Venus involuntarily

squeezing her eyes shut, experiencing a black-out that doesn't quite happen; for the action of shutting out only produces a greater sense of 'mutiny' within. The extremity of what has been beheld cannot be withheld or contained, and she opens her eyes, which suddenly, like a spotlight, illuminate the scene with all the garish force and erotic manner of a baroque painting by Caravaggio:

> And, being opened, threw unwilling light
> Upon the wide wound that the boar had trenched
> In his soft flank, whose wonted lily white
> With purple tears that his wound wept was drenched.
> > No flower was nigh, no grass, herb, leaf or weed
> > But stole his blood, and seemed with him to bleed. (ll. 1051–6)

Shakespeare is hardly done with narrating the delusional effects produced by Venus's troubled brain: 'Upon his hurt she looks so steadfastly / That her sight, dazzling, makes the wound seem three'. Nor is he finished with the boar, whose image mutates in Venus's eyes from a figure of urchin-snouted foulness into a strangely 'loving swine' that 'Sheathed unaware the tusk in his soft groin' (l. 1115–16). Critics, especially of late, have not failed to register the homoerotic moment here: 'the coupling of the boar and the boy stands as one of the most graphically sexual figurations in Renaissance poetry of male / male penetration, of tusk in groin, of male body "rooting" male body'. Just so; but spoken by Venus, the scene must also be read as an expression of her (unfulfilled) passion for Adonis, the boar doing to Adonis what Adonis never did to her. The boar becomes her rival lover, the three forming a bizarre triangle of a sort that leaves no one satisfied and one person dead:

> 'Had I been toothed like him I must confess
> With kissing him I should have killed him first;
> But he is dead, and never did he bless
> My youth with his. The more am I accursed.'
> > With this she falleth in the place she stood,
> > And stains her face with his congealèd blood. (ll. 1117–22)

Of course, Venus wasn't 'toothed like him'. For all her masculine impersonations in the poem, we are reminded, for one last time, that she is anatomically female, and in this poem of amorous substitutions and displacements, in which power and desire are always at odds, she can fall down, stain her face with his blood, but she cannot 'kill' in either sense of that word.

Desire's further sublimation

The sense of sexual frustration on Venus's part continues to the poem's end—an ending that has itself seemed abrupt to some readers—finding ever finer representations along the way. Melting like a vapour, Adonis springs up 'a purple flower...chequered with white', thus resembling his earlier self and yet not his earlier self either, of which discrepancy Venus is acutely aware:

> 'Poor flower,' quoth she, 'this was thy father's guise,
> Sweet issue of a more sweet-smelling sire,
> For every little grief to wet his eyes.
> To grow unto himself was his desire,
>   And so 'tis thine; but know it is as good
>   To wither in my breast as in his blood.' (ll. 1177–82)

The sublimation of desire continues in Venus's metamorphosis into a maternal figure, a mater dolorosa, which includes not just placing the flower in her breast, but her pitiable recognition that 'to grow unto himself was his desire'. Pity then mutates into pathos:

> 'Lo, in this hollow cradle take thy rest:
> My throbbing heart shall rock thee day and night.
>   There shall not be one minute in an hour
>   Wherein I will not kiss my sweet love's flower.' (ll. 1185–8)

And finally pathos mutates into Paphos, the city in Cyprus sacred to Venus, where she 'Means to immure herself and not be seen'

(l. 1194). 'Away she hies', or hurries. The word reminds us, touchingly, of the poem's beginning, in which 'Rose-cheeked Adonis hied him to the chase', but also of how much has metamorphosed in between.

Venus and Adonis is a poem of exuberant passions and small consolations. For Venus, nothing productive comes from love except an anonymous flower (not even the named anemone as in Ovid); and yet for the reader perhaps there is something more if we think of the flower as a figure for the poem, a chequered, or variegated flower of mixed passion as a first offering in print by a now-named author. We should also recall that *Venus and Adonis* is explicitly a poem about beginnings, in this instance (and in keeping with the *Metamorphoses* more generally) an etiology or explanation about the origins of love as 'Sorrow' (ll. 1135–64). In this regard, the poem marks the beginning of, while also prophesying, the author's exfoliation as a poet, his metamorphosis, that is, into the poet of 'some graver labour' mentioned in the dedication to Wriothesley: Shakespeare, the poet of the sorrowful *Lucrece*.

As a foundational poem, traces of *Venus and Adonis* will persist in Shakespeare's later work. Venus herself metamorphoses into Cleopatra (at the very least) in *Antony and Cleopatra*, perhaps even crossing over into Falstaff in all her verbal amplitude in *1 and 2 Henry 4*, and into Helena in *All's Well that Ends Well*, as the stubborn wooer of the callow Adonis-like Bertram. Adonis will also mutate into the 'fair youth', the 'lovely boy' of the Sonnets, including the calcified aristocrat of Sonnet 94, and the calculating Hal of *1 and 2 Henry 4*, the 'boy' Coriolanus, and, early on at least, the initially curt-spoken Cordelia in *King Lear*. Venus is not one-half of Ted Hughes's 'Goddess of Complete Being', but the poem is richly generative, and Ovid accompanies the dramatist nearly to the end of his career, in Prospero's great valedictory speech to his book in *The Tempest* (5.1.33–57), modelled on *Metamorphoses* 7.265–77. Although over-written in places—Adonis rightly wearies of being compelled to listen, just as Jonson generally wished that Shakespeare had 'blotted a thousand lines'—*Venus and Adonis* marked Shakespeare's energizing entrance into the world of print, as his earliest readers realized.

Chapter 3
The Rape of Lucrece

Context and sources

Only thirteen months after *Venus and Adonis* was registered for publication, the Stationers' Register—the office in charge of regulating publications in Shakespeare's day—entered on 9 May 1594 'a book entituled *the Ravyshement of Lucrece*'. No one has doubted that the reference is to Shakespeare's *Lucrece*, as the title page of his poem declares, or 'the Rape of Lucrece', as the work is called on the top of each page, thus making explicit not just the name of the title character but the principal action of the poem as well. Whether early returns on the success of *Venus and Adonis* tempted Shakespeare into writing yet another, longer, and indeed more serious narrative poem for 'the wiser sort' is difficult to say. But with the theatres still closed, there was much in the 1590s literary culture that would have prompted Shakespeare to pen a poem about 'Lucrece, the chaste', and to do so in verse every bit as florid, dynamic, and self-conscious, as rhetorically patterned as that of *Venus and Adonis*. Book 3 of Spenser's *Faerie Queene* (1590), dedicated to the ageing Virgin Queen herself, was expressly devoted to the Legend of Chastity as a celebration of 'Gloriana'. More immediate in date, form, and genre is Samuel Daniel's *The Complaint of Rosamond* (1592). Daniel's highly readable dramatic monologue participated in a wave of enthusiasm for female complaint poems about wronged women that echoed down the

1590s and beyond, of which Shakespeare's *Lucrece* stood, if not squarely, then still in line with this trend. Andrew Marvell's 'The Nymph Complaining for the Death of Her Faun', written around 1650, would be a late instance, indeed a supreme distillation, of the confessional impulses at work in this genre.

One unusual point bears emphasizing in connection with the publishing circumstances of *Lucrece*: the conspicuous presence of *sententiae* in the 1594 quarto edition, wise sayings initially brought to the reader's attention with quotation marks thought to be provided, or overseen, by Shakespeare. An example: 'Tears harden lust, though marble wear with raining' (l. 560). The tightly wrought, paradoxical sentence was proverbial; a variation appears in *Venus and Adonis* (l. 200), but without any textual highlighting. Such practice is new to *Lucrece*, befitting the forthcoming 'graver labour' hinted at in Shakespeare's dedication to *Venus and Adonis*. It also forges one of several important links with *Hamlet*, the only work of Shakespeare's to exceed *Lucrece* in this respect.

What does the new practice tell us about Shakespeare? Quite possibly that his commercial value was on the rise, his utterances worth not just making but marking. Both *Venus and Adonis* and *Lucrece* would soon appear in more prestigious octavo format alongside other works by Ovid in John Harrison's bookshop in St Paul's churchyard. Perhaps too, as a published author, Shakespeare was now taking greater advantage of the medium of print, even assuming the position of a 'sage sayer', as the rhetorician George Puttenham labelled the practitioner of *sententiae*. In doing so, Shakespeare was seeking a measure of control over how his poem was read and remembered, a venture in which he was to experience immediate success. In *England's Parnassus: or the [choisest] Flowers of our Modern Poets*, the first anthology of English literature and published in 1600, there are more citations (thirty-nine) from *Lucrece* than from any other Shakespeare work. Rather unusual, too, for an anthology, all the Shakespeare quotations are attributed to the author by name.

Shakespeare was appealing to a widespread practice of reading in the early modern period quite different from our own habits with literary texts: valuing books precisely because they included much commonplace wisdom, not because of the peculiarity or originality of their thinking. Not that *Lucrece* isn't highly original, but the idea of commonplace wisdom becomes especially relevant in a poem for which reputation figures so significantly. What sayings will be attached to your name, how you are seen by history, what kind of example you are setting for the future: these are central concerns in the poem and form a large part of the legend itself, as can be glimpsed in a lively Renaissance painting by Lorenzo Lotto (Figure 4). In the painting, a feisty Venetian matron, Lucrezia Valier, holds up a drawing of her namesake, Lucrece, in the act of stabbing herself. On a paper below the drawing appears a defiant line in Latin (from Livy), 'No shame lives in the example of Lucretia'.

4. Lorenzo Lotto, *A Lady with a Drawing of Lucretia*, c.1530–3.

Shakespeare wouldn't have known this portrait, but he could have encountered the familiar story of Lucrece in any number of places: in Livy's *History of Rome*, Ovid's *Fasti*, and in the writings of Dionysius Halicarnassus, a Greek historian and rhetorician living in Rome after the Civil Wars; through the poetry of fellow countrymen John Gower and Geoffrey Chaucer; in recent English translations of Latin classics, such as Livy, by William Painter; or learned commentaries, as in the case of Paulus Marsus's edition of Ovid's *Fasti*, perhaps Shakespeare's handiest source since it included marginal compilations of Livy and Dionysius. In other words, to an educated reader of the time, the tale was within easy reach. The story also attracted the attention of one especially influential interpreter. In the *City of God*, Augustine, a convert to Christianity, questioned the commendatory Roman view of Lucrece's suicide precisely because, in his view, her decision to protect her reputation showed a prideful attachment to worldly concerns, a reading that continued to have adherents well into the 17th century.

How much of Shakespeare's poem is indebted to which particular source has been much debated. The sources have their own particular emphases: Livy's with Roman civic history; Ovid's with the lures of the emotions; Chaucer's with Lucrece's exemplary status as loyal wife. Because the collective 'Legend' belonged to the category of history or tragedy rather than mythology, Shakespeare probably felt less disposed to modifying the tale along the radical lines of *Venus and Adonis*. There is no gender bending here. Instead, he broadened, deepened, and in some instances, updated the known outlines of the story, selecting and expanding what he needed to fit the stylistic and thematic needs of the poem and the expectations of its readers. The result is a poem that precisely reverses the polarities of desire in *Venus and Adonis*. Rather than a young man fruitlessly pursued by a more powerful goddess, a powerful lord pursues and fulfils his desire with a young chaste matron. But the poem also exceeds *Venus and Adonis* in a number of ways since what assumes new import in *Lucrece* is the actions of the mind over the movement of the body. *Lucrece* is a profoundly thoughtful poem, with the poet exploring, as his sources do not, the psyches of both villain and victim in greater depth and concentration than even his experience in the theatre had yet allowed.

Graphic content: reader discretion advised?

Lucrece is not for faint-hearted readers. Even if it doesn't merit a trigger warning, as some might wish for its chronological and geographical kin, the sensationally bloody early Roman play, *Titus Andronicus*, it remains a challenging poem with regard to both the story and the means of telling it. The story involves the brutal rape of Lucrece by Sextus Tarquinius—the son of Lucius Tarquinius, the last legendary king of Rome (534–510 BC)—and its excruciating consequences for the victim. The rape takes place barely one-third of the way into this poem of 1,855 lines; the poem is composed in 'rhyme royal', a complex, seven-line stanza generally reserved for high or heroic subjects, instead of the more common and quicker 'sixains' used in *Venus and Adonis*. *Lucrece* contains few incidents, little movement or 'action', that is, and much talk.

The back-story, in fact, originates in a bragging contest among male warriors. 'Disputation', in the formal sense, is also a key term in the poem. Both Lucrece and Tarquin debate at length the consequences that will follow from rape. After the rape, Lucrece embarks on long stretches of lament that include forensic set pieces in which she rails in vain against Night, Time, and Opportunity. Her anguished post-rape contemplation also features an *ekphrasis*—a vivid description of a work of art within a poem—that connects her suffering to the epic subject of the Trojan war. The ekphrasis elevates a side interest in the visual arts in *Venus and Adonis* into a major event in *Lucrece*, one that assumes, moreover, a reader's familiarity with Homer's foundational saga, *The Iliad*. The narrator, too, occupies a large, complicated place in this poem. Always sympathetic to Lucrece, sometimes defensively so, he clearly distinguishes between villain and victim, and yet he is also alert to the deeper shadows, the personal stains, of the story he is telling. For the first 180 lines he is the poem's only speaker. Venus, by comparison, begins wooing Adonis in the second stanza. *Lucrece* is, on many fronts, simply exhausting. It tends not just to use words, but to use them up, to constantly test the limits of its medium. *Caveat Lector*. Reader beware.

And yet for all its challenges, a poem that was said to please 'the wiser sort' at the end of the 16th century continues to do so in the early decades of the 21st. *Lucrece*, writes a recent editor, 'is now one of the most exhaustively discussed poems in the English language'. (There's that word 'exhausting' again.) The critical revaluation is largely owing, although not limited to, a surge of interest in the poem by feminist scholars from the early 1980s onwards: an interest not just in the immediate circumstances of the rape and the fate of the heroine, whether her suicide should be read, à la Lorenzo Lotto's painting, as a triumphant demonstration of her *will*—a key word in the poem—in an unequivocally patriarchal world, but also (and counterpoised to this view) the degree to which the violence done to her is subsumed and therefore contained by a larger historical narrative, which still leaves women on the margins of the republic that Lucrece's suicide is said to initiate. We might regard Venus's outspoken sexuality as temporarily liberating, a breath of fresh air let out in the green world of the countryside, as often happens in Shakespeare's comedy, but the liberation is also a limited, private excursion disconnected from the larger world of politics. *Lucrece*, by contrast, painfully insists that we view the private in light of the public. The two spheres co-exist yet impinge on each other—with disastrous results: for Lucrece, when Tarquin penetrates her inner-space, her closet, and for Tarquin when Lucrece eventually emerges to extract a promise of revenge from her local community.

Visualizing the legend

We can see these strongly juxtaposed attitudes toward public and private space—and the critical implications they entail for a reading of this poem—in several paintings from the rich pictorial tradition associated with Lucrece in the Renaissance. On the one hand, Botticelli's famous painting, *The Tragedy of Lucretia* (1496–1501), offers a coolly realized, carefully structured, panoramic view of events (Figure 5). We see the rape and the personal suffering of Lucrece in the outer, private, enclosed, architectural wings of the painting, while the larger central space is devoted to the public stir caused by her death. Lucrece's corpse, still bearing the knife, stretches out horizontally. She is on a stone sepulchre surrounded by warriors. In a vertical line directly above her body, on the base of a column, appears the standing, sword-waving figure of Lucius Junius Brutus. As if born from Lucrece's womb, he seems almost afloat in the manner of an avenging angel. The tip of his sword points upward toward a statue of David's defeat of Goliath, itself crowned by a Roman arch. The rape has not been effaced from the painting, but it has been displaced by the larger historical narrative so important to the establishment of Florentine Republicanism.

More than a half-century later, Titian's highly dramatic *Rape of Lucrece* (1568–71), on the other hand, focuses only on the moment of Tarquin's attack in the private, claustrophobic world of Lucrece's closet (Figure 6). The room is overstuffed with bedding and pillows; a thick velvety curtain hangs on the back wall, but is parted in the lower left not to let in light but to reveal another viewer—a second viewer, since the act of voyeurism represented here mirrors our own. We peer into an intimate space belonging to a wealthy household only to see its occupant utterly helpless to defend herself. Her vulnerability is set off, in fact, by her lack of clothing, and the positioning of their bodies, especially Tarquin's knee, furthers, from a male perspective, the eroticization of violence in the painting. Compared to Botticelli's rationalized

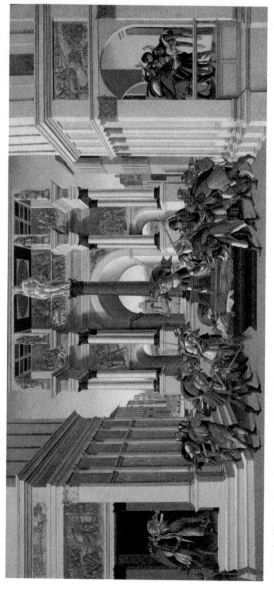

5. Botticelli, *The Tragedy of Lucretia*, c.1496–1501.

6. *Tarquin and Lucretia*, *c.*1571, Titian (Tiziano Vecellio) (*c.*1488–1576).

sense of space, Titian's private world is fraught with energy, emotion, and danger.

Like Botticelli, Shakespeare attends to the wider Roman frame. The poem concludes with Brutus plucking 'the knife from Lucrece's side', and thus taking charge, while putting on something of a Machiavellian disguise even as he throws off his old role as a fool, which he used to escape notice by the Tarquins. Shakespeare, recently the dramatist of the arch-Machiavellian play *Richard III*, adds significantly to his sources here, as Brutus quickly rallies the immediate crowd ('Courageous Romans'). Together, they show Lucrece's

> bleeding body thorough Rome,
> And so to publish Tarquin's foul offence;
> Which being done, with speedy diligence,
> The Romans plausibly did give consent
> To Tarquin's everlasting banishment.

These are the efficient final words of the poem. The emphasis on showing her 'bleeding body thorough Rome' points to Shakespeare's interest in theatrical spectacle in the poem, captured likewise in the suggestion that the Romans applaud the action while giving consent to the plausibility of banishing the Tarquins. At the same time, the use of 'publish' hints at a meaning coming into being with regard to our modern use of publication and the related concept of 'authorship'. Lucrece's displayed body as a publication of Tarquin's wrongdoing forges a sympathetic bond between the reader of the poem and its writer and heroine, who both undertake acts of mutual composition. Earlier we have been told that she gathers 'paper, ink, and pen' to write a letter to her lord (l. 1289). By ending the poem with the publication of the private within the public sphere, Shakespeare invites us to think of the wide reception space for the historical matter of his poem, matter, in fact, to be realized more fully still in the historical sequel when Brutus's ancestor, Marcus Brutus, will appear on centre stage in *Julius Caesar*. Performed at The Globe in 1599, the year the theatre opened, it will feature the spectacle of another bleeding body—that of Caesar's—now, ironically, turned against the Republicans by Mark Antony.

To make the Roman frame of the poem still more visible, Shakespeare, or the printer, also included a prose 'Argument' at the beginning of the poem, largely indebted to Livy. The 'Argument' gives the genealogy of the evil Tarquins, names the principals, and summarizes the actions, beginning with the wager made by the warriors regarding the behaviour of their wives. It refers, in closing, to the political alteration brought about by Lucrece's suicide, in which 'the state government changed from kings to consuls'—a reference not just to the banishment of the Tarquins, in other words. Literary scholars, although by no means all, have found support here for Shakespeare's nascent Republican sympathies. The matter, however, is complicated on a number of fronts, including the possibility that Shakespeare might not have written 'The Argument'; the recognition that evidence of Republican thinking in England at this point is scarce; and the view that political discussions within the poem, most notably by Lucrece, hinge on the distinction between good and bad monarchs, not on replacing one form of government with another. But if the poem touches a hot button in Elizabethan England, with its ageing monarch and pressing worries about succession, it is also the case that Shakespeare's chief interest lies with the interior story of the rape: its motivations and consequences, including Lucrece's swan-like struggle to voice her private history to a wider audience (ll. 1604–60). In fact, Shakespeare differs from his immediate sources in no greater way than in exploring the world as Lucrece might have experienced it. We see as if through a window how Tarquin comes to 'eye' her, and what she thinks, says, sees, and does in response.

Getting down to business

The poem begins, as with *Venus and Adonis*, in *medias res*, likewise densely woven but made of a different fabric, not tipped toward the elegiac but smouldering with erotic force:

> From the besiegèd Ardea all in post,
> Borne by the trustless wings of false desire,
> Lust-breathèd Tarquin leaves the Roman host,

And to Collatium bears the lightless fire,
Which, in pale embers hid, lurks to aspire
　　And girdle with embracing flames the waist
　　Of Collatine's fair love, Lucrece the chaste.

In this poem, so compressed is time and space that it is worth getting our geographical and temporal bearings at the outset. The ancient city of Ardea, referred to here, lies about 20 miles south of Rome, not far from the Mediterranean. When the poem opens (*c*.510 BC), Ardea had been long under attack by the Romans, led by its king, Lucius Tarquinius Superbus. His son is the Tarquin mentioned in line 3. The no longer extant town of Collatium, in line 4, where Lucrece resides, lies about 10 miles northeast of Rome and is governed by Lucrece's husband Collatine. (Somewhat confusingly, and problematically, his name is Lucius Tarquinius Collatinus.)

Intensely compacted too is the poem's language. Ardea sounds like ardour, an association that will soon be developed in the parallel between Tarquin's attack on the besieged city and his attack on Lucrece's chastity, which is then echoed and further complicated in the story of Troy's sacking in the ekphrastic portion of the poem. In the reference here to speed and lust, the poem's 'wiser sort' might also recall that 'rape' and 'rapid' share a common stem in the Latin *rapere*. Time is always a large preoccupation with Shakespeare. In this case, pivoting as events do around the rape, time is experienced subjectively as relentless passion by 'Lust-breathèd Tarquin', and then as unending lament by the ravished Lucrece until grief is given final closure through her suicide. At which point, time abruptly mutates from private, subjective experience to dynastic matters, as the knife used by Lucrece against herself (as an extension of the wound done to her by Tarquin) is plucked from her side by Brutus, who then, in the company of the other mourners, seals an oath for revenge by kissing 'the fatal knife'.

The stanza also introduces the first of the poem's many unusual linguistic contortions in the oxymoron 'lightless fire'. At first, because of the presence of 'bear', the phrase seems to suggest that Tarquin is carrying a torch to guide him through the night, and many have read the passage this way. But Shakespeare never actually mentions the time of day or the distance travelled because he has something else in mind in this poem. 'Lightless fire' serves as a metaphor for Tarquin's lust: passion without benefit of reason or light—the interior ember impatiently lurking, waiting to burst forth in a flame that will girdle and embrace Lucrece's 'waist', her girdle. Try reading this stanza as a 'sixain' by eliminating the extra rhyme line, 'Which, in pale embers hid, lurks to aspire', and you'll see the diminution in force—or more positively, the force 'lurking' in the extra line and in the unholy trinity of rhymes now linking 'desire' and 'fire' with 'aspire'. (The word 'lurks' will also make several significant reappearances later in the poem.) This is a torch, in other words, that Tarquin carries with him wherever he goes, whatever time of day or night, and it can be ignited at a moment's touch: 'As from this cold flint I enforced this fire, / So Lucrece must I force to my desire' (ll. 181–2). These are the chilling words, his motto, as he prepares to march down the corridor to her room.

Tarquin is a ticking time bomb waiting to explode (I came, I saw, I conquered), an inglorious soldier ultimately willing to bring shame to himself and his family for 'a dream, a breath, a froth of fleeting joy' (l. 212). His thoughts have been inflamed, the narrator tells us early on, by Lucrece's beauty, thus setting the stage for the flammable role the eye will play in the poem, in which even tear drops are spectacularly likened to 'balls of quenchless fire' that burn Troy (l. 1554). But Tarquin's ardour has also been stimulated by the ear: by hearing 'praise' of Lucrece's celebrated chastity from her husband, Collatine. Shakespeare tells us this early on too, thus foregrounding an interest in the poem's medium and the complex role of language in communicating desire. Language does not just stimulate lust but also must suffice in the more challenging task of expiating lust's residue, as Lucrece will discover.

Tarquin's reference to a husband's 'praise' of his woman imports a dose of male rivalry into the poem and suggests an element of foolishness, if not culpability, on Collatine's part for 'publishing' what he should have kept unknown, private. Although not a cuckold (because Lucrece is not seduced, although the topic of cuckoldry is raised by Tarquin), Collatine is indirectly responsible for the bad that happens but not for what is restored at the end. Literary scholars have often underscored the patriarchal structure of Lucrece's world, reinforced by Lucrece's unwavering loyalty and references to her 'precious' chastity. Nevertheless, it's hard to read this poem, especially the extensive mourning contest at the end between father and husband over the body of the dead Lucrece, and think that Shakespeare is completely in league with a proprietary view of women—or at least of Lucrece—upheld by the dominant Roman culture. Although never renouncing her place as Collatine's wife, she is given ample opportunity to speak to us as readers, even if not to the Roman public figured in the poem.

Tarquin is a familiar type of the Renaissance warrior, rhetorically sophisticated but brutal. In his ambition to best Collatine and possess the crown jewel of Lucrece's chastity, he resembles the many aspirants of Shakespeare's early history plays, who will readily kill a king to wear a crown, grander villains such as Marlowe's world-beating Tamburlaine in relentless pursuit of the sweet fruition of an earthly crown, as well as Shakespeare's own politically ambitious Macbeth, who will allude to 'Tarquin's ravishing strides' on his way to killing Duncan. In the Scottish play, written a decade later, Shakespeare may well have been recalling his earlier representation of the 'stealthy pace' of Tarquin's movements along the corridor toward Lucrece's chamber in the poem since the scene constitutes one of the poem's more graphically memorable moments. But, if so, it is with a difference.

The dramatist repurposes the reference to fit the hectic pace and context of a play whose sexualized and murderous action unravels ahead of its protagonist, whereas at this point in the poem, Tarquin hardly strides but rather creeps down the corridor, almost frozen with fear over the shame that will accrue to him and his descendants for his actions. Like Macbeth, he rehearses many arguments against the deed, but Tarquin is a creature of his will, his flesh. His actions are frequently likened to those of a beast or bird of prey. He is a graceless reprobate, to summon a few of the anachronistic labels from the theological discourse of the period; and this language of reprobation in the poem infuses shame with a sense of sin, and thus deepens the opposition between devil and saint.

Just as Tarquin is the prototypical warrior, Lucrece is a variation on a Renaissance type of the ideal wife. She is chaste and obedient but not, as we discover, silent. Her early identity, in fact, is that of a 'true type' of the 'loyal wife' before the fall, an identity painfully recollected only after she has been 'rifled' by Tarquin (ll. 1047–50). So chaste is her thinking that innocence cannot discern evil. The habit will change only under the intense emotional pressure experienced while viewing the story of Troy's fall. Early on, as in the 'golden age' (l. 60), her modesty and her beauty—her white blushes and her red—are as one; and yet the two colours are also defenceless, indeed not so much deeply interlocked as rather tensely viewing each other. Thus, in a sense, they are also always looking in the wrong direction, failing to see the danger that lurks: 'The sov'reignty of either being so great / That oft they interchange each other's seat' (ll. 69–70). Lucrece is the lamb to Tarquin's wolf, again to reprise some of the biblical tropes that thicken the evil atmosphere without turning the poem into religious allegory. Her fort is defenceless, to switch metaphors yet again. As we quickly discover, in what amounts to one of several displacements for the sexual act, Tarquin penetrates her private chambers with ease. The grating door, the lock, and especially the foreboding appearance of Lucrece's glove in the rushes—all these

57

'lets' are only momentary stays against confusion that fuel the fire of Tarquin's desire and ultimately makes Lucrece a 'castaway' to herself and to Collatine.

Lucrece's chambers

Time seems all but frozen when Tarquin arrives at Lucrece's inner chambers, the poem's crucial episode. (Shakespeare in *Cymbeline* 2.2, but from a more elegantly seductive perspective and with a different outcome too, will later recall the scene.) Here, as in Titian's painting, all feels overwrought. The scene is highly, indeed overly, theatrical, introduced with a vision of Tarquin 'rolling his greedy eye-balls in his head' (l. 368). In contrast to Titian's depiction of the rape scene, in which the viewer is being given a private showing—and made aware of it through the image of the other viewer lifting the curtain—here we see Tarquin rapaciously viewing Lucrece. We even watch him draw the curtain to look at her eyes. Shakespeare gives us an instance of what feminist philosophers sometimes call a representation of sexual objectification rather than a sexually objectifying representation. We are looking at Lucrece being objectified rather than looking at her body itself as a sexual object. The effect is distancing and disturbing at once, as if we are seeing the scene through Tarquin's 'greedy eyes' and yet often find the view of Lucrece blurred or partially blocked, in the manner of an actor obstructing a sight-line to the stage.

Take the (in)famous depiction of Lucrece's breasts:

> Her breasts, like ivory globes, circled with blue,
> A pair of maiden worlds unconquerèd:
> Save of their lord no bearing yoke they knew,
> And him by oath they truly honourèd.
> These worlds in Tarquin new ambition bred,
>   Who like a foul usurper went about
>   From this fair throne to heave the owner out. (ll. 407–13)

The images quickly yield a variety of thoughts, but none consistently erotic, as the ample weight of scholarly footnotes will testify, in contrast, say, to the 'deer park simile' from *Venus and Adonis*. Indeed, in the next stanza Shakespeare turns to the subject of annotation itself and thus further interrupts a potentially erotic scene—the notorious 'male gaze'—by underscoring the pulsating mechanics of Tarquin's pounding heart:

> What could he see, but mightily he noted?
> What did he note, but strongly he desirèd?
> What he beheld, on that he firmly doted,
> And in his will his wilful eye he tirèd.
> With more than admiration he admirèd
> > Her azure veins, her alabaster skin,
> > Her coral lips, her snow-white dimpled chin. (ll. 414–20)

The Rape of Lucrece

We might note (indeed, how can we not?) the deliberate rhetorical effect of climbing a staircase of desire with each recurring 'What'. Feeling his rising desire in the rhetoric, we know that Tarquin is dangerous, and yet by precisely annotating the passions as he does, Shakespeare redirects our attention away from Lucrece's body and toward Tarquin's, as the usurper-cum-merchant sums up the value of what a 'greedy eye' sees. To him she is alabaster, costly, and in more ways than he understands at the present moment, since his own fall, as 'a captive victor that hath lost in gain' (l. 730), is directly implicated in hers.

Shakespeare's poem, particularly the 300 or so lines leading up to the rape, presents Tarquin's crime as a failure of seduction, the ensuing violence a sign of sexual frustration itself. As in his great Sonnet 129, Shakespeare is more interested in anatomizing the 'rage of lust' (l. 424) than the erotic potential of the story, which often appears in the visual tradition. In Sonnet 129, sex is 'enjoyed no sooner but despisèd straight', and *Lucrece* similarly foregrounds the bleak ironies and illusory nature of pleasure that desire fuels. The possibilities for seduction further dissipate through talk: Tarquin's persuasion tactics mix *carpe diem* formulae with blunt threats of force that will bring shame to Lucrece and her family, including a proposition to kill a slave and place the body in her bed. To these graceless points, Lucrece responds, with 'modest eloquence'—a term that is itself unusual if not paradoxical—about how Tarquin's behaviour will be 'read' by others as befitting a tyrant rather than a king. She is whistling in the dark, of course, as she taps into a familiar line of valued commonplaces from political philosophy in the Renaissance. Indeed, had Tarquin even half an ear open to her argument, he wouldn't be where he is in the first place—in her bedroom. Although the disputation is an exercise in word fencing, the speeches are not empty of meaning. They reinforce a number of important points in the poem, especially regarding the place of shame in Roman culture as applicable to Elizabethan interests. More significant still for Lucrece, in thinking outside the bedroom, in bringing larger matters of politics to bear on personal behaviour, she hints at the outspoken woman she will become.

The rape scene itself is highly condensed, visually muddled, as it had to be, something akin to a filmic blur in the unusual shifts of the imagery, but leaving us with little doubt about what has transpired:

> The wolf hath seized his prey; the poor lamb cries,
>> Till with her own white fleece her voice controlled
>> Entombs her outcry in her lips' sweet fold.
>
> For with the nightly linen that she wears
> He pens her piteous clamours in her head,
> Cooling his hot face in the chastest tears
> That ever modest eyes with sorrow shed.
> O that prone lust should stain so pure a bed!
>> The spots whereof, could weeping purify,
>> Her tears should drop on them perpetually. (ll. 677–86)

The white fleece is, we discover, not a reference to lamb's wool but a metaphor for the bed sheet enwrapping her mouth and thus preventing Lucrece from crying out. Some have viewed the reference to 'her lips sweet fold' as the scene of sexual violation itself, and her inability to cry out is thus accorded a yet more primal meaning in the process.

The entangling repression continues, as the reference to clothing shifts to her nightly linen and the entombed outcry now becomes 'piteous clamours in her head', multiplied and relocated from the body to the mind or psyche, where, in some sense, it will remain for the duration of the poem. We also discover that the agent of entanglement is Tarquin; and again Shakespeare displaces the sexual act, this time through the reference to her chaste tears cooling his hot face. And yet again, the extra rhyme line carries an additional burden of meaning with its jolting apostrophe—now the disbelieving narrator arrives on the scene—and the horizontal reduction of Tarquin to 'prone lust' and Lucrece to a once pure but now 'stained' bed.

Still, Shakespeare's language is more than sufficient. The matter of Lucrece's being stained will quickly become the subject of her thoughts, indeed, the only subject in all its ramifying power, while Tarquin will shortly disappear from the poem, a shadow of what he was, except as he will figure into Lucrece's thinking.

> He, like a thievish dog creeps sadly thence;
> She, like a wearied lamb lies panting there.
> He scowls and hates himself for his offence;
> She, desperate, with her nails her flesh doth tear.
> He faintly flies, sweating with guilty fear;
>   She stays exclaiming on the direful night.
>   He runs and chides his vanished loathed delight. (ll. 736–42)

This is highly patterned rhetoric, a series of brilliantly lit comparisons. The parallelisms assert their now common bond of shame, the antitheses, their different responses to their new circumstance. She stays, he runs; this is her poem, not his.

'Herself herself detest'

More than 1,000 lines separate the rape of Lucrece from her suicide, a rather astonishing gulf to navigate. In Livy and Ovid, and in the poem's 'Argument', a grieving Lucrece quickly dispatches a messenger to summon Collatine as a means to enact revenge. In Shakespeare's poem, however, showing the influence of Daniel's *The Complaint of Rosamond*, grief opens into a huge wound, underscoring the crisis Lucrece has suffered now that she no longer possesses the single identity she once had as Collatine's chaste wife, a time when body and soul were equally dear (l. 1163). This inward stretching of the sources might well remind us of Hamlet's own labyrinthine quest for revenge—and also of the comparable role that the ekphrasis will play in the process, as both plots of death hinge, to a degree, on insets centring on the fall of Troy.

But, of course, their stories differ significantly, as do their means of telling. Hamlet's is about determining the veracity of the Ghost's story; it is largely, indeed nearly unfathomably, epistemological in nature. Lucrece's is about expiation and endurance, resistance and fortitude, confirming a charge of rape and refuting a charge of adultery. If never quite overcoming her self-detestation over her polluted condition, except through suicide, she nonetheless acquires a sense of agency, of *will*. Her will is literalized in her resolve to make 'an abridgement' to the 'will' that Collatine is asked to 'oversee' (ll. 1198–210) and furthered through her authorial preoccupation with acquiring the tools of writing, in which she manifests the heightened frenzy associated with literary 'invention' by male poets of the period (ll. 1290–1302). Her suicidal need is made especially acute by the lingering suspicions, too, that she has been made pregnant by Tarquin: 'This bastard graff shall never come to growth: / He shall not boast who did thy stock pollute, / That thou [Collatine] art doting father of his fruit' (ll. 1062–4). She also refuses to find easy relief from her distress in the apparently comforting belief, spoken by the surrounding Roman community, that 'her body's stain her mind untainted clears' (l. 1710). For Lucrece, there is no easy separation of body and soul, no comforting dualism allowing for transcendence. Purgation is by way of the body—specifically by the hand holding a pen, and then a dagger—but as directed by the mind.

Although we have already noted that *Lucrece* is a poem about thinking rather than acting, we might still ask in this particular instance why Shakespeare didn't cut to the chase, having Lucrece quickly commit suicide in the manner of his sources? One answer is that Lucrece's interiority is made visible through her 'complaints'. These expressions arising from her unstable mind provide an important thematic balance to Tarquin's obsession with her body. Lucrece's great complaint against 'Misshapen Time', culminating in her curse against Tarquin (ll. 918–1020); her sense of isolation; her need for finding a companion to ease her suffering in the mythical figure of the raped Philomela; her sense of acute shame over how she might be represented in history, whether by nurse, orator, or 'feast-finding minstrels' (l. 817)—together help to give voice to the rape victim's trauma, something all but denied the maimed Lavinia in *Titus Andronicus* by the very nature of the horrific crimes done to her body, in which her tongue is cut out and hands lopped off.

In this regard, Lucrece's invocation to Philomela, 'Come, Philomel, that sing'st of ravishment: / Make thy sad grove in my dishevelled hair', assumes a special meaning not available to the ravished Lavinia. It is an example of how shared song can create a sense of female companionship that sharpens a sense of the woe done to each (ll. 1128–48). Misery also has a special affinity for mournful song. The poem explains, 'Distress likes dumps [mournful songs or plaints] when time is kept with tears' (l. 1127). The remark, strange to modern ears, was proverbial in Shakespeare's day, and marked as such in the 1594 text. Keeping time with tears is a way to recalculate the burden time has become.

Depicting the fall of Troy

A more pointed and revealing series of vocalizations occurs with the ekphrastic episode recounting the Fall of Troy: 'that she her plaints a little while doth stay, / Pausing for means to mourn some newer way' (ll. 1364–5). More pointed because the 'newer way', marking Shakespeare's own significant entrance into the emerging literary field of ekphrasis, deliberately sets off the sounds of speech—Lucrece's voice in particular—against the silence of painting, and more revealing because the epic scale of the 'well-painted' action stimulates a stronger, more passionate set of responses in Lucrece than pastoral recollections of Philomela can accomplish. So moved, in fact, is Lucrece by the pictorial representation of Hecuba's silent woes, in which 'the painter had anatomized / Time's ruin, beauty's wrack, and grim care's reign' (ll. 1450–1) that Lucrece intervenes on Hecuba's behalf and, in effect, assumes a yet larger more active role for herself:

> 'Poor instrument,' quoth she, 'without a sound,
> I'll tune thy woes with my lamenting tongue,
> And drop sweet balm in Priam's painted wound,
> And rail on Pyrrhus that hath done him wrong,
> And with my tears quench Troy that burns so long,
>   And with my knife scratch out the angry eyes
>   Of all the Greeks that are thine enemies.' (ll. 1464–70)

And so intense is her identification with sacked Troy and its victims that she demands that the painting do more than the painting (but not the poetry) can do—to produce the cause of grief:

> 'Show me the strumpet that began this stir
> That with my nails her beauty I may tear:

Thy heat of lust, fond Paris, did incur
This load of wrath that burning Troy doth bear;
The eye kindled the fire that burneth here,
   And here in Troy, for trespass of thine eye,
   The sire, the son, the dame, and daughter die.' (ll. 1471–7)

Lucrece is speaking, of course, about Helen of Troy, whose
abduction by Paris is often referred to as a rape, and is so earlier
by the narrator (l. 1369). But not here by Lucrece, who wishes to
distance herself as far as possible from the person, in her mind,
whom she also most closely resembles. Her violent responses
prompted by a work of art—scratching and tearing, with knife
and finger nails—can be read therapeutically, as expressing at
one remove her outrage over the violence she has suffered, but
also masochistically, as directed against that other part of herself
that stimulated Tarquin: her beauty.

Lucrece's climactic response to the painting centres on the figure
of Sinon, the Greek traitor, whose guise of innocence allowed
him to penetrate Troy's walls. Initially, the painter's wondrous art
tricks Lucrece into thinking Sinon innocent because she can only
imagine 'so fair a form lodged not a mind so ill' (l. 1530). Then, in
the manner of a dark epiphany, Lucrece comes to see otherwise,
in what is the most grammatically complicated act of reflection in
the poem:

   'It cannot be,' quoth she, 'that so much guile'—
   She would have said 'can lurk in such a look,'
   But Tarquin's shape came in her mind the while,
   And from her tongue 'can lurk' from 'cannot' took.
   'It cannot be' she in that sense forsook,
      And turned it thus: 'It cannot be, I find,
      But such a face should bear a wicked mind.' (ll. 1534–40)

It is as much the process as the conclusion that captures our
attention, as if she is revisiting the moment itself when Tarquin's

shadowy shape came into her chamber, the earlier memory now seen as breaking through the present moment, involuntarily recalled in the manner of a traumatic event. Indeed, for us as well, for the reflection seems teased into being by the reference to 'lurk' first encountered in the poem's opening stanza, and the sonic proximity that now obtains between 'lurk' and 'look', with the two words bearing their stealthy connection into the open. As soon as say 'lurk' and Tarquin's 'look' appears.

To Lucrece, the appearance of the innocent 'face' is seen to belie the reality of the 'wicked mind'. More than all her apostrophes to Night, her willed turn of phrase here marks perhaps her fullest recognition of dark knowledge or wisdom, captured in the taut parallels linking her circumstances with those of Priam:

> 'To me came Tarquin armèd to beguild
> With outward honesty, but yet defiled
>> With inward vice: as Priam him did cherish
>> So did I Tarquin; so my Troy did perish.' (ll. 1544–7)

And she utters a sentiment that will run through *King Lear*: 'Priam, why art though old and yet not wise?'. Not older than Priam but certainly wiser, Lucrece unleashes—and expends—her fury at Sinon/Tarquin. The most interesting moment is perhaps her own recognition 'at last', accompanied by a knowing smile, of the folly of her actions, enabled, and yet rendered useless, by the artificial circumstances of the ekphrasis:

> Here all enraged such passion her assails
> That patience is quite beaten from her breast.
> She tears the senseless Sinon with her nails,
> Comparing him to that unhappy guest
> Whose deed hath made herself herself detest.
>> At last she smilingly with this gives o'er:
>> 'Fool, fool,' quoth she, 'his wounds will not be sore.' (ll. 1562–8)

Lucrece as Roman tragedy

Painting, as with song, as with idle words, offers only limited comfort for Lucrece. Each creates a pause, a show of discontent, no sooner indulged than left behind as inadequate, collapsing in advance of the action and therefore preparing us and Lucrece for her final act. But each is valuable nonetheless for presenting a complex, sympathetic character, not simply a stoic, let alone an avenger, although Lucrece has aspects of both. In her capacity for reflection, she anticipates Hamlet; and as Hamlet has a foil in Laertes, so Lucrece does in Brutus of early Rome. Brutus chastises Collatine for being slow to accept the challenge of revenge, and in doing so badly mischaracterizes Lucrece: 'Thy wretched wife mistook the matter so, / To slay herself that should have slain her foe' (1826–7).

No doubt some might prefer Brutus's solution: that the victim retaliates. Retaliation is surely easier, as the efficient phrasing suggests, but along with its misogynistic slur, Brutus's reading of the situation also reduces Lucrece to an avenger without understanding her struggle. He cannot grasp the dilemma that she alone has explored: an understanding that the mind can be perfectly persuaded that it did not consent to the event itself and yet still feel that the body is contaminated, burdened with its 'load of lust'. To that end, her bleeding body, majestic in its ruination, likened to 'a late-sacked island, / Bare and unpeopled', offers vivid proof of her divided condition, for which purgation is only possible by a knife:

> And, bubbling from her breast, it doth divide
> In two slow rivers, that the crimson blood
> Circles her body in on every side,
> Who, like a late-sacked island, vastly stood
> Bare and unpeopled in this fearful flood.
>> Some of her blood still pure and red remained,
>> And some looked black, and that false Tarquin stained. (ll. 1736–43)

Lucrece's death provokes many curiosities. I mentioned earlier Augustine's condemnation of it as an act of suicide that revealed too great an attachment to the world and her reputation. Within the poem, her suicide sets off an unseemly grieving competition between father and husband, whose apparent excess reminds us, if we needed reminding, how much this poem is about the mimetic properties of language. Their exaggerated representation of their grief points to how words stimulate, structure, and in this instance, impede action, but only for a moment, since their own 'emulation', or competition, initiates a desire by Brutus to throw off his disguise and take control of the situation.

The scene is profoundly theatrical, in sharp contrast to the end of *Venus and Adonis* where Venus is left to mourn her deceased love in a private space. A curiosity in himself, Brutus has been playing the fool in order to fly under the Tyrant King's radar, as it were. It is also a markedly 'Roman' moment. The words 'Rome' and 'Roman' suddenly redound throughout the closing stanzas. They receive their most emphatic stipulation in the great vow Brutus declaims:

> 'Now, by the Capitol that we adore,
> And by this chaste blood so unjustly stainèd,
> By heaven's fair sun that breeds the fat earth's store,
> By all our country rights in Rome maintainèd
> And by chaste Lucrece's soul that late complainèd
>   Her wrongs to us, and by this bloody knife,
>   We will revenge the death of this true wife.'

Brutus's is a binding oath, forcefully displacing, in the name of Rome, the many earlier chivalric vows in the poem, including Lucrece's own quaint wish that 'Knights by their oaths should right poor ladies' harms', a sentiment that seems certainly more appropriate for *The Faerie Queene* or the genre of the complaint than Roman Tragedy. The foundation of the Republic is a greater matter, and it requires a greater pledge.

The narrator now comes forth, in Brutus's footsteps (not shadow), to spell out the scene in full theatrical detail, as if encoding stage directions to the players for how the scene should be acted:

> This said, he struck his hand upon his breast,
> And kissed the fatal knife to end his vow;
> And to his protestation urged the rest,
> Who, wond'ring at him, did his words allow.
> Then jointly to the ground their knees they bow,
>   And that deep vow which Brutus made before
>   He doth again repeat, and that they swore.

Was Shakespeare hungering to return to the stage or simply utilizing its imaginary properties for his reader's full benefit? It's impossible to know. But as his last published poem for some years to come, *Lucrece* closes on a strong note of avowal. Shortly after it was entered into the Stationers' Register in May, in the summer of 1594, Shakespeare was to join the Lord Chamberlain's Men, to be renamed the King's Men under James, and for whom he worked until he retired from the theatre altogether.

As with *Venus and Adonis*, *Lucrece* provided Shakespeare with a storehouse of personifications that were to be embodied on stage in a variety of characters. It also had a long, if somewhat different, reach into the playwright's career. *Lucrece* begs to be read in light of Shakespeare's Roman plays. It is a refinement on *Titus Andronicus* in almost every respect, a distant historical link to *Julius Caesar*, a preparation for both *Hamlet* and *Antony and Cleopatra*. The poem also offers a 'source' for *Macbeth* and *Cymbeline*, as already suggested, and, in its marked temporality, the galloping pace of eros, it forms an interesting point of comparison with *Romeo and Juliet*, written shortly thereafter. Small domestic scenes, such as Lucrece with her sympathizing servants—her weeping maid (ll. 1212–95) and her loyal groom (ll. 1338–58)—remind us, as well, of similar moments in *Othello* and *Lear*; and if Lucrece's unbending loyalty toward her husband points in the direction of Desdemona, her decision to commit suicide hints at an affiliation with Othello and bespeaks a general concern with reputation throughout Shakespeare, including, in particular, the 'slander' that is said to kill Hero in *Much Ado About Nothing*. Oddly, the many critical books written about Shakespeare's women often leave Lucrece off the list, no doubt a feature reflecting the usual modern preference of plays over poems; and yet *Lucrece* is the only work by Shakespeare to have a woman's name appear alone in the title. Her status as a tragic heroine did nothing less than open up this grander avenue for women for the duration of Shakespeare's career.

Chapter 4
On first looking into Shakespeare's *Sonnets*

Setting forth

After the publication of *Lucrece* in 1594, Shakespeare went underground, in a manner of speaking, as a writer of poems. Not that he became invisible. In fact, the opposite is the case. Shakespeare returned to the theatre and began writing a series of plays in the mid-1590s for his acting company, the Lord Chamberlain's Men, which included *Romeo and Juliet*, *A Midsummer Night's Dream*, *Richard II*, and *Love's Labour's Lost*. All are works of great poetic versatility and formal variety. *Richard II* is set entirely in verse, while several, attending to the fashion of the day, weave sonnets and lyrics into the play's dramatic action.

The poet continued in the drama, but his activity as a writer of poems for publication, of sonnets in particular, remains largely shrouded in darkness. The historical record does tell us a few important things. Thanks to the contemporary testimony of the Cambridge educated schoolmaster, Francis Meres, in *Palladis Tamia, Wits Treasury* (1598), we know that at least some of Shakespeare's 'sugared sonnets' were circulating among his 'private friends' in the 1590s. And a few poems appeared in *The Passionate Pilgrim* (1598 or 1599), a collection of poems cobbled together by the piratical William Jaggard, who was seeking to capitalize on Shakespeare's growing reputation as poet and dramatist. The book's title, followed by the author's name ('W Shakespeare'), was probably intended to recall the extended sonnet in *Romeo and Juliet* when the lead characters first meet (1.5. 90–107). The collection prints versions of Sonnets 138 and 144, in conjunction with three other 'sonnets' from *Love's Labour's Lost*, although they appear without attributed authorship and amidst other poems by various (again unidentified) hands. But apart from these few references, we know, with certainty, precious little else about the specific origins of Shakespeare's *Sonnets*, a book that would eventually garner more critical attention than any other single book of poems published in English.

Puzzles and problems

Shakespeare's *Sonnets* are generally regarded as the finest collection of sonnets in the English language, and this chapter will seek to offer yet one more perspective on why this is so. But after 400 years, puzzles continue to abound, and while some notable critics want to dismiss them as irrelevant, we ought to be aware of the more important ones before 'setting forth'—to adopt the language from the 1609 dedication page (Figure 7). Although Shakespeare's authorship of the *Sonnets* has never been seriously questioned—the title page declares '*SHAKE-SPEARES SONNETS* / Never before Imprinted', with the title appearing on the running head of every page—the dedication seems designed to perplex the reader. And perplex it does, perhaps in keeping with the general tenor of sonnet sequences of the period in which speculation regarding biographical incidents and the details of courtship was part of the genre. (Sidney's *Astrophel and Stella*, first published in 1591, is exemplary in this regard; *Berryman's Sonnets*, by the American poet, John Berryman, continues the game well into the 20th century.) The precise meaning of the opening address 'to the onlie begetter', for instance, is only the first puzzle. Does it mean 'source of inspiration', in the manner of a muse figure or lover? Or

TO.THE.ONLIE.BEGETTER.OF.
THESE.INSVING.SONNETS.
M^r.W.H. ALL.HAPPINESSE.
AND.THAT.ETERNITIE.
PROMISED.

BY.

OVR.EVER-LIVING.POET.

WISHETH.

THE.WELL-WISHING.
ADVENTVRER.IN.
SETTING.
FORTH.

T. T.

7. **Dedication to *Shake-speares Sonnets*, 1609.**

does it refer, more distantly, to the person in possession of the manuscript, written by 'Our Ever Living Poet'? And who is the grammatical subject of the phrase, the person referred to with the mysterious initials 'Mr. W. H.'?

Hypotheses abound here, some more fanciful than others, as does much amateur sleuthing. The two leading, but by no means sole, contenders are: William Herbert, the third Earl of Pembroke, in Jacobean circles the greatest patron of his generation and one of the persons to whom the Folio *Works* is dedicated; and, by reversing the initials, Henry Wriothesley, third Earl of Southampton, the often painted, androgynous icon of the 1590s, whom we've already met as the dedicatee of the narrative poems in Chapter 2. Or as Oscar Wilde ingeniously argued in *The Portrait of Mr. W. H.* (1889), might the reference be to an actor named Willie Hughes, perhaps hinted at in Sonnet 20 in the line 'A man in hue, all hues in his controlling'? And is the dedicatee, whoever he is, the same person as the addressee in the poems, or rather addressees, since some, but perhaps not all, of the first 126 Sonnets are directed to an unnamed young man (or several young men?) of higher social standing than the poet and often referred to by critics as the 'fair youth'? And then, to look altogether beyond the dedication page for a moment, what sense are we to make of the later series of poems, beginning with Sonnet 127, including the famous Sonnet 130 ('My mistress' eyes are nothing like the sun'), spoken to or about a woman now infamously known as the 'dark lady'? Is she, too, a real person? And if so, is she brown-skinned or black, Italianate or African, someone perhaps Shakespeare met in London, or rather a literary convention, again as found in Sidney? To no one's surprise, many possibilities have been put forward. Some, like Mary Fitton, later identified in a portrait to be 'fair'—a word that, like 'black', can equate complexion with moral behaviour—have dropped by the wayside. The candidate *du jour* is Aemelia Bassano Lanyer, or Lanier, not because there is any firm evidence linking the two. In this Lanyer is like all the other possibilities. She fits the bill because she was of Italian descent, bore a child to Henry Carey (the Lord Chamberlain and Shakespeare's patron), and was an able poet and musician—the first woman poet in English, in fact, to publish a book of poems. Her life, in relation to Shakespeare's, if not a matter of proof, is material for fiction, and recently treated as such by Mary Sharratt in *The Dark Lady's Mask: A Novel of Shakespeare's Muse* (2016).

In addition to readers' never-dying fascination with interpreting the Sonnets as a sort of *roman à clef*, we also have reason to wonder about the publisher 'T.T.', Thomas Thorpe. Although his identity is not in question, the little we know of his character allows for a range of possible responses. Once regarded as an unscrupulous opportunist, Thorpe has since been accorded greater respect as a reliable publisher of important books (Jonson's *Volpone* for one, in 1605). But it is also true that he was not always squeaky clean in his dealings with literary property of the period, and we are still unsure how he managed to acquire the manuscript of Shakespeare's poems. Furthermore, we cannot know to what degree, if at all, Shakespeare was involved in the publication of the Sonnets that he authored. Did Thorpe acquire, surreptitiously, a manuscript version of the Sonnets, to which Shakespeare then gave his general consent to publish? Or did Shakespeare travel from Stratford (where he is speculated to have worked) to supply Thorpe with a copy himself sometime around 1609? Or did some third party—W. H. are also the initials of Shakespeare's brother-in-law (William Hathaway)—serve as intermediary, leaving the 45-year-old poet at enough of a remove to let his awkwardly juvenile Sonnet 145, his wooing sonnet to Anne, survive?

If the question of authorial involvement evades a firm answer, the complex matter of dating the Sonnets has led to some valuable (albeit again debatable) surmises. While it is generally assumed that the Sonnets were a product of the 1590s, when sonnet writing was at the height of fashion, further 'stylometric' arguments based on the frequent occurrence of rare words found in early and late Shakespeare have posited a more intricate, and in some instances surprising view of things. The later numbered Sonnets, 127–54, those involving the 'dark lady', were (it is believed) not written last but first, perhaps helping to explain their unusual rawness in places; the earlier numbered poems, 1–60, are thought to have been composed later in the decade, c.1595–6, and Sonnets 104–26 later still, apparently extending into the Jacobean period. Further fine tuning of possible composition dates involves other groups or sequences and includes speculation about Shakespeare's habits of revision, but there is little consensus about when Shakespeare might have stopped either revising or writing sonnets altogether—perhaps by 1604? Or was he tinkering with them right up to the date of publication? Sonnet 126, addressed to 'my lovely boy', is markedly incomplete, as if the printer were still waiting for the author to supply a final couplet. And in between the early and later dates where might fall the composition of many individual sonnets? The dates proposed, for instance, regarding one of the more insistently occasional poems, the so-called 'mortal moon' Sonnet (107), range from an improbably early 1579 to a more likely post-Elizabethan 1604.

Regardless of when we might date a specific sonnet or a sequence of sonnets, what are a few takeaways here for a general reader? First, in contrast to many of his Elizabethan competitors—Drayton is the major exception—the long gestation period itself reflects a restlessness on Shakespeare's part to continue exploring a form of expression independent of the need to meet a tight theatrical schedule. Second, the order of the *Sonnets* in the 1609 Quarto does not reflect the order of their composition, thus casting further doubt on the novelistic practice of reading the sequence as a straightforward reflection of Shakespeare's love-life, the kind of reading popular in the 19th century and that continues in many quarters today. Nonetheless, it does not follow that the Sonnets are purely fictive addresses, with no basis in reality. The 'dyer's hand' Sonnet (111), touched on in Chapter 1, gives the lie to this view, as do any number of sonnets that seem partially situated in the social and dramatic fabric of the day. Third, readers should be prepared to look not just at but between sonnets, as the poems often participate in a larger series of dramatized situations. Not all sonnets do so, as we'll see in our discussion of Sonnet 116, but many 'self-refer', or pick up threads found elsewhere in the volume, sometimes in the immediate vicinity, at other points some distance away. The dedication hints at one of these through lines when it refers to 'That Eternity Promised by our Ever-Living Poet', and thereby calls attention to a major (Elizabethan) concern with immortalizing the lover through verse (e.g. Sonnets 18, 19, 55, 60, 63, 81, 101). Overall, whatever the dates involving the composition of individual poems, the 1609 title page, *SHAKE-SPEARES SONNETS / Never before Imprinted*, reminds us that we're considering one author's special place within a wide literary tradition.

As with *Venus and Adonis* and *The Rape of Lucrece*, the *Sonnets* raises issues that have received considerable attention in the last several decades: matters of homosexual desire and transsexuality, of gender and racial stereotyping, of temptation and sexual addiction. And they painfully explore the jealousy that arises not just when lovers are separated but when perceived or actual infidelities are thought to occur. Sometimes these matters involve an odd triangle—the three people who are often the subject of the Sonnets: the speaker, a young man, and the 'dark lady', as if art has taken on a life of its own, as it so often did for Shakespeare in the theatre. A central question the Sonnets keep asking, too, is whether it is possible to imagine love, or talk about love, that is not sexual and yet also dateless and worth preserving. And sex, sometimes, of the most potentially degrading order. The poems do so, it bears emphasizing, not as part of a single, overarching story, in the declamatory mode, say, of the narrative poems, but as a series of quieter, uniquely individualized situations and startling revisions within the larger pattern of Petrarchan poetry.

The sonnet form: a brief overview

The sonnet had its beginnings in 13th-century Sicily, at the Norman court of Frederick II, where its fourteen-line structure was initially established, and then soon migrated to Italy. Dante was one of its early practitioners in *La Vita Nuova* (1293–4), mixing sonnets with other songs or canzone, but it gained its popularity under the impress of Francis Petrarch's *Canzoniere* or 'Songbook' (written 1330–74). The 366 poems in the *Canzoniere* praise a woman named Laura, whose name forms a pun on the laurel crown pursued by poets as well as on 'breeze' and 'gold' (in Italian, *l'aura* and *l'auro*). Petrarch's sonnet cycle made the form a pan-European affair, influencing poets in Italy, Spain, France, and, eventually, England to pursue laurels and ladies of their own devising. Its nominal locus was the court, and the poetic production of sonnet cycles, in conjunction with epic, helped to mark a country's cultural coming of age. Both Sir Thomas Wyatt (1503–42) and Sir Philip Sidney (1554–86), two of the poets most associated with the Petrarchan sonnet's transplantation to England, spent extended time in France and Italy.

Literary critics often devote significant attention to describing important technical features typically associated with the different forms, and a little familiarity with the rules improves appreciation for how the game is played. The Italian, or Petrarchan, sonnet often spins its double, 'closed' quatrains out of just two rhymes (rhyming is easier in Italian than English), *abba, abba*. After the eighth line of the octave, there occurs a sharp turn in thought (the *volta*), marked off structurally by a sestet made up of three new rhymes appearing in a variety of patterns (*cde, cde; cd, cd, ee*) and frequently offering a counter-argument or melody—a word that reminds us of the sonnet's association with music or song.

The English, or Shakespearean, sonnet, on the other hand, is modelled on three 'open' quatrains, each with a different pair of rhymes (*abab, cdcd, efef*). Meaning tends to accrete gradually and more prosaically. The quatrains are often logically or temporally connected (when…when…then…as), and the volta (but…, yet…) is shifted downward, from line 9 to line 13, where the turn, the major structural seam in the English sonnet, is marked through a concluding couplet with a rhyme of its own (*gg*). There are also hybrid forms, as we will see in the case of Spenser; and Shakespeare's Sonnets can sometimes behave in the manner of the Petrarchan sonnet and reveal a sharp turn of thought after the eighth line, as we observed in our discussion of Sonnet 33 in Chapter 1. (Other notable instances include Sonnets 18, 29, 44, and the exceptionally pitched shift of 94.) Whatever the form, the Elizabethan sonneteer's subject is most often a profession of love, developing out of a long tradition of epideictic discourse involving praise and blame (including self-blame, of which Shakespeare was its subtle, agonizing master), and often utilizing a grammar of amatory suffering, stock imagery, and familiar situations, again substantially varied and made vigorously explicit by Shakespeare.

At the heart of the form as it came to be practised in the Renaissance is also a central paradox. The commonality of subject matter is invoked to promote the alleged individuality of the speaker and capture a unique moment or event in that person's emotional life. On the one hand, the form possesses an impetus toward the fictional representation of character. On the other hand, the poem's meaning depends upon an element of ritual by aligning itself with recognized forms of experience. (Petrarch aligned his *Canzoniere* with the calendar year.) These include experiences voiced by other poets in the tradition or those the poet has voiced in other poems in the volume or in earlier quatrains of a single poem through marked patterns of repetition. Many Elizabethan sonneteers consequently sound alike. A few do not. Sidney, Spenser, and Shakespeare lead the way in this regard, followed by Samuel Daniel and Michael Drayton, with Shakespeare least indebted, as we shall see, to forms of experience as recounted by lineal descendants of Petrarch. Shakespeare left his special imprint on the page through his signature use of language, which pried open and vastly expanded what had been a deliberately narrow, often precious, courtly grammar. Not only is his vocabulary larger than that of his contemporaries, it is drawn from a wider spectrum of experience. As the Scottish poet

Don Paterson has recently suggested, Shakespeare's originality lay in willfully realizing that '"love" was the one theme capacious enough to encompass every other, and that he needn't stray from its centre.'

Post-Renaissance practitioners of the sonnet—and there are many—greatly widen the parameters of form and subject matter but continue to be drawn to the sonnet as an ideal vehicle for personal expression. The form is long enough to develop an idea in depth, compact enough to require concision of argument, and sufficiently complicated to encourage technical innovation and originality of thought. Few have played the game better than Elizabeth Bishop. Her late, dazzling, little poem called 'Sonnet' (1979), written in loose dimeter verse instead of the usual pentameter line, appears recognizably Petrarchan in structure but now seen anew, indeed upside down in its division of parts and reversed in terms of its movements. An initial six lines (the sestet) is devoted to images of being 'Caught', then followed by eight lines (the octave) recounting the experience of being 'Freed', or 'gay', to cite the poem's last word, a word that reminds us of the sonnet's enduring association with sexual identity. The terms 'Caught' and 'Freed' also point to two different, indeed contradictory, attitudes toward form itself. Some poets seem caught or bound by it, thus enacting or embodying the Procrustes' bed analogy that critics of the form repeatedly levelled against it from the days of Ben Jonson onward. Others, like Shakespeare, do not. As was true with stanzas in the narrative poems, he seems to have owned the form nearly from the outset, perhaps because he had already been practising quatrains and couplets in the narrative poems. 'From fairest creatures we desire increase', he remarks in the opening line of the first sonnet, as if signalling his own capacity to multiply poem after poem, 'That thereby beauty's rose might never die.' A hundred and fifty-three poems later, his mood has darkened, become more complex, but the desire to produce seems undiminished.

Sonnet 116

For many readers of Shakespeare, our introductory questions
regarding the publishing circumstances of the *Sonnets* will have
little bearing on understanding the individual poems per se.
In part, this is because we frequently encounter a Shakespeare
sonnet on its own. But Sonnet 116, the great 'marriage' poem,
seems to exist deliberately independent of temporal concerns. That
is one of its special powers. The sonnet trumpets a love beyond
contingency, even beyond the dynamics of gender fluctuations, a
triumphant note that perhaps inspired a version of the poem to be
set to music by the most gifted of Caroline composers, Milton's
friend and collaborator, Henry Lawes:

> Let me not to the marriage of true minds
> Admit impediments; love is not love
> Which alters when it alteration finds,
> Or bends with the remover to remove.
> O no, it is an ever-fixèd mark,
> That looks on tempests and is never shaken;
> It is the star to every wandering barque,
> Whose worth's unknown, although his height be taken.
> Love's not Time's fool, though rosy lips and cheeks
> Within his bending sickle's compass come.
> Love alters not with his brief hours and weeks,
> But bears it out even to the edge of doom.
>   If this be error and upon me proved,
>   I never writ, nor no man ever loved.

The fact that the poem continues to be performed at weddings
today hints at a timeless connection with ritual. Yet the described
situation might well be a purely hypothetical thought experiment:
what would a marriage of true minds look like? (Shakespeare will
take up the same question in the severely compact 'The Phoenix
and Turtle'.) The poem operates in philosophical mode as it

explores what language we might use to define the meaning of such a union. And it is not the only Renaissance poem invested in this topic. Historically speaking, Sonnet 116 partakes in a minor tradition of late Renaissance or 'metaphysical' poems given to definitions of love, including Donne's 'The Ecstasy' and 'A Valediction: Forbidding Mourning', Edward Herbert's 'Ode on a Question Moved: Whether Love should Continue Forever', and Andrew Marvell's 'A Definition of Love'.

As Shakespeare phrases the matter, a marriage that admits impediments—a resonant word borrowed from the solemnization of matrimony in *The Book of Common Prayer*—would be rocky from the start. Or it would not be true love if it alters just because of alteration (a change in the weather, say, or because of sickness, to echo the marriage rite), or bends because one person is removed or away from the other (out for a walk, overseas, or with another person). The terms are general enough to allow considerable latitude for interpretation; but however rarefied love appears—'it is the star to every wandering barque'—the urgency of address ('Let me not...'), the speaker's absolute sense of conviction ('Love is not love'), seem to deny the premise that the poet is simply producing an abstract definition of love. Rather, like the imprisoned Richard II in the last act of his play, the poet is hammering out his thoughts on a necessary subject, but in this case firmly, with a sense of audience, and with an air of finality sounded in the couplet.

Getting a grasp on this poem means evaluating its diction (the special flavour attached to a bulky word like 'impediments', for instance, or the legalistic implication of 'proved' in the couplet), and the paradox of its quickly shifting imagery ('O no, it is an ever-fixèd mark'). We might also attend to the unusual wrenching of syntax and word order often produced by the necessities of rhyming in English. Line 10 is more readily apprehended if 'come' were to be the first rather than the last word in the line (as in 'rosy lips and cheeks / Come within his bending sickle's compass'). But much would be lost, not only the pronounced alliteration of 'compass come' but also the special force generated by the oddly compounded participial phrase 'bending sickle's compass come', a syncopated quickening of rhythm that Allen Ginsberg especially enjoyed riffing on. As for the progression of thought, we move (or perhaps leap) from quatrain to quatrain, from measuring love in the second quatrain as a mysterious function of distant space to figuring love's resistance to the ominous compass-bearing Time in the third; and then we come to the sonnet's weighty ending and the complex challenge issued in the couplet with regard to the preceding statements.

We might also wish to wait on some finer points of metre and word variation: the emphatic stress on 'fixèd', for instance, and the extravagant use made of 'alter', 'remove', and 'bend' in a poem that values steadfastness. It's possible, of course, on the strength of its repeated assertions, to bend the poem back on itself and read the poem ironically, that is, as overstatement. The subject of love is so severely and absolutely defined that it all but defies human experience. Love that 'bears it out even to the edge of doom' makes love sound, well, a bit unbearable, heroic in the extreme, and yet perhaps still admirable in conjuring up a hint of Christ's sacrifice in the doomsday image. Indeed, there's something unsettling, less than fixed, even vagrant, about concluding a line in which the semantic meaning of a phrase is undercut by the metre, as in the case of 'never shaken' (line 6), with its weak, unstressed extra syllable. At a wedding ceremony, a preacher cannot speak on both sides of the matter, but a poem can entertain more than a single possible meaning. Eminently serviceable, the marriage sonnet also represents a wild fling with words.

Self-reflecting moments and monuments

Nor is its exceptionalism exceptional. There is no single way to read a Shakespeare sonnet although many keys have been offered.

On any given day, we may read a poem differently, so complex is their tone and the meaning. But Sonnet 116 points to a truism often sounded by critics, especially those who came of age in the era of New Criticism shortly after World War II: that a Shakespeare sonnet is 'the essence and exemplar of the poem as the separable, stand-alone thing. Even when a Shakespeare sonnet is part of a sequence, it is there for itself.' Squared off on the page, 'A Sonnet is a moment's monument', to quote a famous definition by the Victorian poet, Dante Gabriel Rossetti. (A late modernist like Bishop might amend that definition to read a 'fleeting, unstable moment'.) And the initial circumstances in which most readers first encounter a Shakespeare sonnet, usually in an anthology, only further underscores its unique, independent status as a poem, re-affirmed often, as in Sonnet 116, with a reflexive account of its own status as having been *written* and, we might add much after the fact, *written* by Shakespeare.

Indeed, no poet in English has ever surpassed Shakespeare in underscoring the persuasive reflexivity of his art, the ennobling nature of the sonnet's power to give life, and therefore the monumentality of his medium in its bid to be remembered. In one form or another, the sentiment provides the conclusion of some of his most famous sonnets. We can see this practice at work in the following roll-call of couplets, each closing the poem with a different rhyme and tone. Sonnet 15: 'And, all in war with Time for love of you, / As he takes from you, I engraft you new'—with the play on 'graft' calling up the Greek word to write, *graphein*. Sonnet 18: 'So long as men can breathe or eyes can see, / So long lives this, and this gives life to thee'. Sonnet 55: 'So, till the judgement that yourself arise, / You live in this, and dwell in lovers' eyes'. Sonnet 60: 'And yet to times in hope my verse shall stand, / Praising thy worth, despite his cruel hand'. And Sonnet 81: 'You still shall live (such virtue hath my pen) / Where breath most breathes, even in the mouths of men'. For now, we'll just note the emphatic use of the present tense in each, a topic which we will explore in more detail in Chapter 5. Shakespeare is not promising fame in the distant future. He is promising 'life' in an ever-expanding present. His friend continues to live through the poet's efforts, and, because of the poem, in the eyes, mouths, and judgement of others.

Shakespeare is not unique in this concern, only in its practice. Any number of contemporary English sonneteers can be found promising to immortalize the beloved: Samuel Daniel, Michael Drayton, and, most notably, Edmund Spenser in his *Amoretti*, first published in 1595. (Sidney was relatively uninterested in this aspect of poetry in his otherwise deliberately artful *Astrophel and Stella*.) Spenser's famous Sonnet 75, for instance, beginning 'One day I wrote her name upon the strand', promises, against the sands of time, to perpetuate his lover's fame and name (as well as his own) through his verse. We might suppose this element of heightened artistic self-consciousness and the appeal to the durability of writing to be peculiar to the Renaissance, a marriage, as it were, of Italian high artistry and German technological innovation in the discovery of the printing press, but we can trace the popular trope of perpetuation of fame through art back to classical poetry. A precedent if not a source for Sonnet 55 can be found in Horace (*Odes*, 3.30) and in Ovid (*Metamorphoses*, 15.983–95, in the Arthur Golding translation), where the power of the classical models helps to propel Shakespeare's sonnet in an altogether different direction from Spenser's poem, away from courtly modesty and toward the monumental claims of art to survive across epochs of time.

Petrarchan oddities

To compare Spenser's and Shakespeare's poems also hints at the wider story of Shakespeare's distance from mainstream Petrarchan interests. Spenser conceives his sonnet within the polite boundaries of the courtly lyric. His poem is especially attentive to the Neoplatonic ladder of love, in which the body is subordinate to the soul, and ideal human love forms a pathway to the divine, albeit not without tension imposed by earthly desires. Part of a longer sequence of eighty-nine poems that works its own twist on Petrarchan conventions by ending happily in marriage, Sonnet 75 proceeds through a series of elegant, perfectly measured exchanges—dance steps in verse quatrains—between the poet and his beloved in decidedly antique diction. The worshipped lady is critical of the poet's 'vain' efforts at immortalizing 'a mortal thing', her name in the sand, with the pun on 'vain' pointing to the self-serving futility of his actions. Challenged by her demurral, the poet in turn rises to a higher order of response by promising fame but fame that will only be fully realized in a future after Judgement Day.

> My verse your vertues rare shall eternize,
> And in the heavens wryte your glorious name:
> Where whenas death shall all the world subdew,
> Our love shall live, and later life renew.

Spenser's unusual practice of interlocking the quatrains through a shared rhyme (*abab, bcbc, cdcd, ee*) reinforces the decorous nature of this sonnet, in which the sound of the 'v' in 'vain' can be re-purposed through the poet's 'verse' to create a link to her 'virtue'. The poem is meant to please, and smoothly please it does.

Shakespeare's Sonnet 55 sounds a completely different note from Spenser's—literally by eschewing Spenser's archaic language, a topic Shakespeare will directly address in Sonnet 106 ('When in the chronicle of wasted time'), and by including harsh phrases like the much annotated 'besmeared with sluttish time'. In Sonnets 129, 135, 136, and 144, Shakespeare takes the concept of coarseness into more graphic, un-Petrarchan territory. But here, confident from the outset, unwavering in rhyme's capacity to praise, the poem captures some of the solemn grandeur of its Latin sources in the slow pace of the regular pentameter verse, as

I have somewhat crudely indicated in the bold, italicized syllables
in the first quatrain:

> Not *mar*ble, *nor* the *gild*ed *mon*u*ments*
> Of *prin*ces **shall** out*live* this *pow'r*ful *rhyme*,
> But *you* shall *shine* more *bright* in *these* con*tents*
> Than *un*swept *stone* be*smeared* with *slut*tish *time*.
> When wasteful war shall statues overturn,
> And broils root out the work of masonry,
> Nor Mars his sword, nor war's quick fire shall burn
> The living record of your memory.
> 'Gainst death and all oblivious enmity
> Shall you pace forth, your praise shall still find room,
> Even in the eyes of all posterity
> That wear this world out to the ending doom.
>   So, till the judgement that yourself arise,
>   You live in this, and dwell in lovers' eyes.

Golding's translation of Ovid reads, in fourteeners: 'Now have
I brought a woork to end which neither Joves feerce wrath, / Nor
swoord, nor fyre, no freating [gnawing] age with all the force it
hath / Are able to abolish quyght [quite]'. Shakespeare takes the
heavily alliterating second line as his point of departure, with its
firm use of negatives to serve as a springboard to describe the
positive aspects of his verse. By way of compression, Shakespeare's
first line also includes Horace's reference in Ode 3.30 to having
built a monument more lasting than bronze ('Exegi monumentum
aere perennius'). Shakespeare's opening gambit is nothing if not
bold, gaudy with alliteration, even promising to make a show
of the person he is praising by claiming that 'you shall shine more
bright in these contents / Than unswept stone besmeared with
sluttish time'.

An unusual comparison, to be sure. The great irony, of course, is
that Shakespeare does not name his lover here or elsewhere in the
Sonnets, although the author will toy with his own name in the

'Will' Sonnets (135, 136) and thus work a wildly indecent change on a Petrarchan convention:

> Whoever hath her wish, thou hast thy *Will*,
> And *Will* to boot, and *Will* in overplus;
> More than enough am I that vex thee still,
> To thy sweet will making addition thus.
> Wilt thou, whose will is large and spacious,
> Not once vouchsafe to hide my will in thine?
> Shall will in others seem right gracious,
> And in my will no fair acceptance shine?
> The sea, all water, yet receives rain still,
> And in abundance addeth to his store;
> So thou, being rich in *Will*, add to thy *Will*
> One will of mine to make thy large Will more.
>   Let 'no' unkind no fair beseechers kill:
>   Think all but one, and me in that one *Will*.

It's hard not to blush over this bit of juvenilia, regardless of when the poem might have been written. No Astrophel, he, a star-gazer of a distantly chaste Stella, Shakespeare is a restlessly indecent rule-breaker. He plays openly with his name, italicized here, as it is in the 1609 Quarto, an unusual practice probably designed to call attention to the author's Christian name, '*Will*', and, we must add, to much else besides, including the variable size of his penis and (from his angle) the woman's indisputably large vagina. Her presumed promiscuity is in keeping with the 'dark lady' sonnets, but her darkness here is an effect of her alleged sexual abundance, not specifically correlated with her ethnicity. His 'will', not always italicized and capitalized in the Quarto, might be taken as a sign of his concern over his rather small place in her presence. The poem looks down, not up, reductive of both male and female sexes, but differently so. '*Will*' has the advantage of speaking, in showing his wit by ringing many changes on his name, including the possibility that she has '*Will* to boot'. (What can this literally mean, one wonders?) Her advantage perhaps is not speaking at all. The whole poem is rudely clownish and certainly a touch pathetic, but weirdly memorable. Shakespeare thought it worth another poem on the same subject.

To return to more serious structural matters raised by Sonnet 55, the quatrain, the basic unit of thought in a sonnet, also functions very differently in Spenser and Shakespeare. Spenser's careful linkages have little place in Shakespeare. Each quatrain in Sonnet 55, for instance, functions independently, energized by its own distinct grammar, syntax, and imagery: Not...; When...; 'Gainst...; So...'. The parts are held together by a wide range of ideas associated with time and wastage, including the reiterated promise of what poetry can do against time in something like an escalation of its signifying power. I have always found the third quatrain both daring and terribly moving. Shakespeare encourages us to imagine the addressee's sudden active movement—the sign of his coming to life, and not just being a 'living record of memory'—in the image of his 'pacing forth'. It's the kind of animation through art that occurs on a larger scale in the marvellous fifth act of *The Winter's Tale*, when, "Gainst death', Hermione slowly begins to move, but here the illusion is created on the page, in the room that is a stanza, in fact, according to Italian translation.

Shakespeare's interest in the poet's immortalizing power of verse seems more a legacy of the page than the stage. In Shakespeare's plays poets are rarely represented with much dignity or power. Cinna, the poet, is beaten to death because of his bad verses in *Julius Caesar*. Theseus likens the poet, in his madness, to the lunatic and the lover in his famous speech in the fifth act of *A Midsummer Night's Dream*. Nor is the poet's power necessarily a legacy of the printed page either, since none of Shakespeare's references in the Sonnets requires the fixity of print as part of the condition of their being long lasting. As with so much else in the Sonnets, the sentiments seem enabled by the limited, perhaps even intimate, circumstances of their address as poems that initially circulated among his 'private friends'.

Shakespeare is willing to boast about his art, as it were, *sotto voce*, just as he will go further, and more deeply, into the private subject of sexuality than any other sonneteer of the period, perhaps any other poet in English. When we think of its small circle of addressees, we do not hear declamation as uttered by the Soul of the Age for All Time (as Ben Jonson remarked in publicly eulogizing the Shakespeare of the First Folio). We hear carefully nuanced speech to another listener, the reference to the Last Judgement in the concluding couplet of Sonnet 55, indeed, quietly qualifying the poet's claims. As Shakespeare says, in Sonnet 81, 'Your monument shall be my gentle verse'. And his verse is even more 'gentle' and self-effacing when he thinks of his own death in Sonnet 71. 'No longer mourn for me when I am dead.' The opening line could hardly be plainer, the sonnet as structurally uncomplicated as it is emotionally direct.

Although not always 'gentle' or genteel, especially in the 'dark lady' sonnets, the adjective helps to locate a strain frequently sounded in his verse and which Jonson and other contemporaries frequently associated with the person. In Sonnet 87, the poet quietly puts a good face on things:

> Farewell, thou art too dear for my possessing,
> And like enough thou know'st thy estimate.
> The charter of thy worth gives thee releasing:
> My bonds in thee are all determinate.
> For how do I hold thee but by thy granting,
> And for that riches where is my deserving?
> The cause of this fair gift in me is wanting,
> And so my patent back again is swerving.
> Thyself thou gav'st, thy own worth then not knowing,
> Or me, to whom thou gav'st it, else mistaking;
> So thy great gift, upon misprision growing,

> Comes home again, on better judgement making.
> Thus have I had thee as a dream doth flatter:
> In sleep a king, but waking no such matter.

Sonnet 87 has sometimes been seen to mark an end to Shakespeare's relationship with the 'fair youth', except, of course, the collection continues on, reminding us that lyric is not dependent on narrative in order to represent the finality of loss. Note, too, that the sonnet is not explicitly gendered. Its power, rather, comes from voicing the moment in all its emotional richness, which in this poem develops (again) out of a single word in the first line—'dear'—that carries with it the double sense of being 'lovely' and 'expensive', indeed too expensive, too rich, and thus pointing again to the class difference separating lover from beloved. The first line speaks of costs, all borne by the speaker. As the poem develops, the sonnet requires of the reader a detailed understanding of Elizabethan property law to trace out all the twists and turns of their relationship—I am reminded of Don Paterson's claim that for Shakespeare '"love" was the one theme capacious enough to encompass every other'—except for one basic fact that cannot be rationalized away and doesn't require glossing. The speaker is the injured party. He is the one being left, as the first line makes amply clear and the couplet clearer still in voicing the delusional nature of his passion by imagining the social hierarchy upside down and himself, like Bottom in *A Midsummer Night's Dream*, momentarily 'a king'. We hear it also in the dying fall of the extra syllable, the weak ending sounded at the outset and repeated thereafter in all but the second and fourth lines.

One of the most 'gentle' sonnets is also one of the oddest in its structure. A particularly exquisite complaint, Sonnet 126 is singular for being in couplets and, as I mentioned earlier, curiously lacking a final pair of rhyme lines. Yet even without its final lines, it brings to a close the poems to the young man or 'fair youth' with a warning:

> O thou my lovely boy, who in thy power
> Dost hold Time's fickle glass, his sickle hour;

Who hast by waning grown, and therein show'st
Thy lovers withering as thy sweet self grow'st—
If Nature (sovereign mistress over wrack)
As thou goest onwards still will pluck thee back,
She keeps thee to this purpose, that her skill
May Time disgrace, and wretched minutes kill.
Yet fear her, O thou minion of her pleasure:
She may detain, but not still keep, her treasure!
Her audit (though delayed) answered must be,
And her quietus is to render thee.

(   )
(   )

Here we immediately register the addressee's gender. The apparently older, wiser speaker argues that Nature confronts 'Time's fickle glass, his sickle hour' on behalf of the 'lovely boy'. As beauty's cosmetician, Nature keeps the boy in his youthful glow in an effort to disgrace Time.

She will lose, of course, although not without putting up a motherly struggle for her creation. The play with fickle glass / sickle hour also couldn't be finer. Time controls both, as holder of vanity's mirror and as ultimate weed whacker. In the 1609 Quarto, 'f' and 's' are even orthographically identical. But nothing tops the strangeness of the conclusion. Why are those parentheses there? What do they signify? Are they authorial or editorial? Is something missing from an original manuscript? Or are they pointing to the something that is missing, to what Wallace Stevens would one day riddlingly describe at the end of 'The Snow Man' as 'the nothing that is not there and the nothing that is'. Their love which no longer is.

Chapter 5

Further patterns and irruptions in the *Sonnets*

Along with the passions they voice, there are important recurring motifs in the *Sonnets*, lending a special rhythm to the whole. One of the most resonant is one we've just witnessed in our discussion of Sonnet 126 in Chapter 4: that of Time's inexorable march ('When I do count the clock that tells the time'—Sonnet 12); of seasonal change and human mutability, movingly combined together, for instance, in Sonnets 73 ('That time of year thou mayst in me behold') and 97 ('How like a winter hath my absence been'); and of the corruptibility of relationships, of bonds. After the great rendering of joy in Sonnet 18 ('Shall I compare thee to a summer's day?'), re-sounded in the measured assurance of Sonnet 29 ('When in disgrace with Fortune and men's eyes'), we discover the acute sense of shame and pain, of self-lacerations and rationalizations in the face of rejection, of the speaker doing violence to himself in front of others: 'Alas 'tis true, I have gone here and there, / And made myself a motley to the view, / Gored mine own thoughts, sold cheap what is most dear, / Made old offences of affections new' (110). In these lacerating self-depictions, we might recall Caravaggio's visually gruesome, famous painting of *David with the Head of the Giant Goliath* in the Villa Borghese Gallery in Rome. The artist—by extension the poet—has rendered a grisly portrait of himself in the decapitated (gored) image of the older giant's head being held by the attractive, partially dressed, fair youth.

In tracing the vicissitudes of the speaker's love and fortune, many readers will likewise discover threads and patterns linking local groups of poems together. Some are sufficiently visible and continuous to form small sequences, such as the opening eighteen Sonnets in which the poet, borrowing a subject found in Erasmus, urges the young man to marry. The so-called 'rival poet' sequence (Sonnets 78–86) is another example, where Shakespeare, confessing writer's block, squares off against other contenders for the young man's affections. 'Was it the proud full sail of his great verse, / Bound for the prize of all-too-precious you, / That did my ripe thoughts in my brain inhearse, / Making their tomb the womb wherein they grew?' (86). In doing so, Shakespeare gives local habitation and thought to the kind of rivalry that, among dedicated Petrarchists like Sidney, for instance, feels more airy than real. In Shakespeare, the confrontation is such that we want actual names. Marlowe? Chapman? Jonson?

Shakespeare's two loves

There is also the further, related matter of the strange, painful love plot that shadows the whole. First mentioned in Sonnets 40–3, a triangle emerges linking the poet, the young man (or men), and the 'dark lady' in an unseemly and, to the speaker, an especially humiliating relationship. The material seems more appropriate for the stage—think *Othello*, for example—than for a book of Elizabethan sonnets written in the footsteps of Petrarch. For all their reputed sugariness, life and love in Shakespeare's Sonnets keep welling up from below, bringing the sour along with the sweet, especially when Shakespeare returns to the subject of triangular infidelity in Sonnet 144, 'Two loves I have, of comfort and despair', one of the sonnets printed earlier in *The Passionate Pilgrim*.

> Two loves I have, of comfort and despair,
> Which like two spirits do suggest me still.
> The better angel is a man right fair;

The worser spirit a woman coloured ill.
To win me soon to hell my female evil
Tempteth my better angel from my side,
And would corrupt my saint to be a devil,
Wooing his purity with her foul pride.
And whether that my angel be turned fiend
Suspect I may, yet not directly tell,
But being both from me, both to each friend,
I guess one angel in another's hell.
    Yet this shall I ne'er know, but live in doubt,
    Till my bad angel fire my good one out.

The dramatic inter-involvement of good and evil in this poem might remind us of a similar situation as described in a contemporary sonnet by Michael Drayton, beginning 'An evil spirit your beauty haunts me'. But what is essentially an allegorical device in Drayton is only quasi-allegorical in Shakespeare. Shakespeare's sonnet is a quickly struck, complex drama of suggestion and doubt, a three-dimensional entanglement featuring, as it often does in his Sonnets, doubt and suspicion, and captured at the outset in the loaded, complex use of the word 'suggest' (to prompt, tempt, or seduce a person to evil, as well as not to state overtly or know absolutely). The poem concludes only when the tryst is known by the speaker to be decisively over at some point in an imagined future beyond the poem. Until then, like some unhinged Othello without ocular proof, he can only guess what might be going on between his two friends.

The sonnet also picks up the misogynistic thread in the 'Will' Sonnet (135), now re-calculated and particularized to include a third person—a good angel—and the possibility of his secret cohabitation with the woman, now 'coloured ill'. The key line, in this regard, is one of several sharpened in the Quarto version: 'But being both from me, both to each friend', phrasing that emphasizes his isolation from them. (The line from *The Passionate Pilgrim* version reads, less precisely, 'For being both to me, both to each, friend'.) In terms that mingle theological with sexual judgements, his 'good angel' has perhaps converted, turned to the 'evil side', leaving the speaker in a limbo of doubt and self-hate. The evil side, while introduced in the first line as one of 'Two loves I have', is explicitly associated with 'hell' in the third quatrain, a synonym elsewhere in Shakespeare for vagina. The final image of his better angel being fired out has acquired much commentary, as we might readily imagine, including the possibility that 'fire' represents venereal disease, a theme that reappears in the final two 'Anacreontic' Sonnets 153 and 154, modelled on a poem from the Greek Anthology. The speaker of 144 has much to regret, and regret it is he sounds, fully and deeply, in the great, neighbouring Sonnet 147, beginning 'My love is as a fever, longing still / For that which longer nurseth the disease'.

Individual irruptions

So suggestive, in fact, are the circumstances described here (and elsewhere) that readers will be forever tempted to posit a 'story' for the Sonnets. But if there is a larger story, it is of interest because it is realized in the particular, which is not to say that the Sonnets altogether lack an element of narrative but that narrative is embedded in the recognition of newly intense emotional exchanges and changes in the imagined relationship. Sonnet 33, discussed in Chapter 1, is one such marked moment, a moment when the speaker first entertains doubt about his lover's fidelity. An even sequentially earlier irruption occurs in Sonnet 13. The voice of Erasmian avuncular wisdom, addressing the 'tender churl' with regard to his civil responsibilities to marry and propagate, is suddenly abandoned, and a new one is born in the vocative of a poet infatuated by the object of his address: 'O that you were yourself; but, love, you are / No longer yours than you yourself here live'. It's as if Polonius has been suddenly displaced by Romeo, and a new understanding of lyric is discovered.

Sonnet 20, the 'master-mistress' Sonnet, has long possessed an especially heady place in this saga of passion's irruption. Here is the poem, with its teasing use of feminine rhymes throughout:

> A woman's face with nature's own hand painted,
> Hast thou, the master mistress of my passion;
> A woman's gentle heart, but not acquainted
> With shifting change as is false women's fashion;
> An eye more bright than theirs, less false in rolling,
> Gilding the object whereupon it gazeth;
> A man in hue, all hues in his controlling,
> Which steals men's eyes and women's souls amazeth.
> And for a woman wert thou first created,
> Till Nature as she wrought thee fell a-doting,
> And by addition me of thee defeated,
> By adding one thing to my purpose nothing.
>> But since she pricked thee out for women's pleasure,
>> Mine be thy love, and thy love's use their treasure.

Comparisons with cross-dressing in the theatre are inevitable: in Shakespeare's day, boys dressed up to play the parts of women, who then, in the case of Rosalind in *As You Like It* and Viola in *Twelfth Night*, play the parts of young men, etc. The Sonnet raises explicitly the question of same-sex desire, already encountered by us in the bisexual 'two loves' of Sonnet 144, by positing the addressee as androgynous. The master mistress is a precursor, of sorts, to today's biologically realized transsexual: in this case, he was originally formed by Nature to be female until lovingly changed to male and therefore possesses qualities of both. Earlier generations of readers tended to read a heteronormative relationship into the Sonnets by capitalizing on Renaissance habits of Platonizing male friendship. Fewer readers today rehearse this argument. They prefer, rather, to underscore the homo-erotic attraction represented by the young man who, in this poem, clearly inspires the speaker's 'passion', dominates his thinking, and lures him into a forest of ardour involving double-entendres with misogynistic shadings.

As the final line makes clear, though, both Neoplatonic and erotic readings remain active in the juxtaposition of 'thy love'—the Neoplatonic idealizing sentiment—with 'thy love's use', the specific anatomical instrument Nature pricked out. We see the author, at least a Neoplatonist by default, looking simultaneously upwards and downward, at the perfected ideal and at his passionate desire. Critics can sometimes become overly solemn about sexuality in Shakespeare's Sonnets—as could Shakespeare himself in his great sermon on the intoxicating power of lust in Sonnet 129—or, alternatively, overly zealous in seeking out every possible sexual nuance imaginable. Sonnet 20 puts us a bit on our toes on both fronts. Amid the frisson, it's important not to miss the lightness of touch that comes with inventing an Ovidian fable about Nature's smitten reaction to the young man's beauty, one that, happily, doesn't lead to destruction on this occasion. This rose-cheeked Adonis lives on, providing pleasure for both men and women, although a different kind to each.

Intensity

Why do we feel the speaker's situation in the Sonnets so intimately and intensely? One answer, and it could have been noted almost anywhere in our discussion of the Sonnets, is what critics of lyric poetry generally refer to as 'real time'. The sonnet's brief action is always in the present. Even when the speaker is remembering a past event, the reader performs, or re-performs, the speaker's thoughts in the present, as in the famous instance of the Proustian Sonnet 30, beginning 'When to the sessions of sweet silent thought / I summon up remembrance of things past'. All those 'things past' are, in fact, doubly present—to the speaker in the use of the present tense verb ('I sigh the lack of many a thing I sought'), and to the reader, who stands in for the speaker summoning 'things past'. In the narrative poems, time is a feature of dialogue and dramatic action. Time can be foreshortened or lengthened at any point to fit the larger story; we observe and admire the handling of incident. But in the Sonnets, it is almost always a matter of our speaking the circumstances audibly to ourselves, not simply, as in the case of a soliloquy on the stage, listening at some remove to someone mouth the words in the first person, but rather performing the words ourselves. That condition of intimacy is often made yet more intricate and immediate through Shakespeare's quietly insistent use of the first person pronoun 'I' and a 'you' or 'thou' who can also be 'us', the reader.

The most celebrated instance in the Sonnets—indeed one of the most celebrated in all English poetry—of our being invited to be both the speaker's silent participant and his addressee is Sonnet 73.

> That time of year thou mayst in me behold
> When yellow leaves, or none, or few, do hang
> Upon those boughs which shake against the cold,
> Bare ruined choirs, where late the sweet birds sang.
> In me thou seest the twilight of such day
> As after sunset fadeth in the west,
> Which by and by black night doth take away,
> Death's second self, that seals up all in rest.
> In me thou seest the glowing of such fire
> That on the ashes of his youth doth lie,
> As the death-bed whereon it must expire,
> Consumed with that which it was nourished by.
>   This thou perceiv'st, which makes thy love more strong,
>   To love that well, which thou must leave ere long.

The sonnet begins with a gesture toward narrative ('That time of year'), as if we're about to be told a story, but shifts quickly into lyric self-address. With each quatrain, in the repetition of the deictic formula, 'in me thou', the sonnet engages in an increasingly intimate ritual describing the speaker's ageing person, first in light of seasonal (autumnal) change, then in terms of daily (twilight) time, and finally in the context of his imminent death (total darkness). We are drawn into the act of voicing change as it appears to another—not into an ever-closer view or image of the person speaking. The poem is extraordinarily elusive in that regard. We discover instead an unusual drift in the metaphors used in each quatrain to simulate the ageing speaker's mind as well as a rather marked, fuzzy use of relative pronouns ('that', 'this', 'which').

Keats's famous comment about the Sonnets seems right on the mark here: 'I neer found so many beauties in the Sonnets—they seem to be full of fine things said unintentionally—in the intensity of working out conceits'. The conceit involving the line, 'Bare, ruined choirs, where late the sweet birds sang', is among the finest, most intriguing in all of Shakespeare. The speaker's drifting thoughts, as represented in the figure of the birds on branches, then likened to choristers at the time of the dissolution of the monasteries, seem on the brink of expiration. They are taken to the extreme in the gorgeous imagery here and in each subsequent stanza, only to be pulled back from the edge in the strongly worded, admonitory couplet, which binds like a covenant:

> This thou perceiv'st, which makes thy love more strong,
> To love that well, which thou must leave ere long.

Part of the surprise here is the sudden reversal. The addressee, not the speaker, is the one who 'must leave ere long'. The addressee, in this case, is also the reader who has reached the end of the poem only to become acutely aware of its temporality, its imagined disappearance. Imagined, of course, because the poem on the page can always be re-performed, or revised, as the opening lines of the next poem quietly remind us:

> But be contented when that fell arrest
> Without all bail shall carry me away;
> My life hath in this line some interest,
> Which for memorial still with thee shall stay.

Now it is the poet's turn to assess and represent the effects of his death, 'that fell arrest', on another.

Going forward

Many of the poems discussed or touched on in this chapter are among the more frequently anthologized of Shakespeare's Sonnets; and while the individual poems are often too thick with meaning to constitute a browser's paradise, readers should be encouraged to go off-grid and forage on their own. W. H. Auden thought there were forty-nine poems that were 'excellent throughout', approximately one in three, but he leaves open which these might be, as well he should. Tastes vary as does the experience of reading itself, especially of poems as rhetorically intricate as these. To paraphrase Hamlet, the Sonnets have that within which passes show. A poem that can sometimes sound tender, at other times might seem more ironic and bitter, the moods fluctuating under the pressure of concentration. The poems we most prize at one point in our lives are also not necessarily the ones we most value at another time—their poetic range is no less than seeming to speak to all ages in the cycle of life. And as Shakespeare's plays have been sometimes credited with inventing the human, so the Sonnets have been sometimes seen as inventing subjectivity. Whether either claim is true is perhaps less important than recognizing that both speak to the fullness of representation at work on the stage and the page. If they are not the greatest sonnets in any language, it is only because they were not among the first and most influential. That laurel belongs to Petrarch.

As for the more immediate traces left by the Sonnets on the drama, these are more difficult to track than with the narrative poems, not just because the Sonnets lack the comparable exploration of character types but also because they are less datable. The writing—or at least the thinking and revising—of them seems coterminous with many of the plays and much of Shakespeare's dramatic career. As a result, we tend to project back onto the

Sonnets, sometimes rather loosely, the voices, moods, and situations we find in the plays. Their inwardness is like Hamlet's; their infatuation like Romeo's or Juliet's; their ageing speaker's worship of the young man who disappoints like Falstaff and Hal in the *Henry 4* plays or Antonio and Bassanio in *The Merchant of Venice*; their acutely rendered jealousies like those experienced in *Othello* and *The Winter's Tale*; their sophisticated, mannered lying like that of Antony and Cleopatra. And we tend to project onto the plays images and conceits found in the Sonnets. A reader who knows both the plays and the Sonnets well will find no end of crossovers, even if it is difficult to speak directly of 'influence'. The phrase, "Tis better to be vile than vile esteemèd', could be the opening of a soliloquy, for instance, perhaps spoken by Iago, but it is, in fact, the first line of Sonnet 121.

With regard to the afterlife of the Sonnets as sources of influence, this, too, is a rich subject that has attracted many, but it can only be touched on here. Keats's name has already been mentioned. Wordsworth, as well, famously remarked in 'Scorn not the Sonnet' that 'with this key / Shakespeare unlocked his heart'. But however important he was in creating a general taste for the sonnet, which languished through much of the 18th century, it was Milton, not Shakespeare, who most influenced Wordsworth in form and diction, in public stance and utterance, as was generally true for the sonneteers preceding him, like Charlotte Smith. By contrast, Keats was more receptive to both 'closed' and 'open' forms of the sonnet, Petrarchan and Shakespearean. Although he was later to disband with both on the way to discovering the more capacious stanzaic form used in his Odes, he did so only after having written 'When I have fears'. That sonnet almost perfectly enacts the patterned arc and inward thinking often found in Shakespeare, even if its melancholic couplet departs in mood from Shakespeare's usual endings.

The Victorian period is so saturated with Shakespeare—the poet, the dramatist, and, perhaps above all, the Stratfordian person as

England's national poet—that it is sometimes difficult to separate out individual strands of influence. Vexingly so, because early Victorians inherited and wrestled with Malone's fellow-editor, George Steevens, and his disgust over the sexual indeterminacy of Sonnet 20, the theme of male friendship in the Sonnets more generally, and the baroque language in which the subject was expressed. Nonetheless, sonnets in the period abound, as do sonnet cycles. The latter appeared under the partial impress of Shakespeare in enumerating and exploring, in extended form, the multiplying significance of love and the acute awareness of subjectivity that accompanies this experience. The best-known sequences are Elizabeth Barrett Browning, *Sonnets from the Portuguese* (1850), George Meredith's *Modern Love* (1862), and Dante Gabriel Rossetti, *The House of Life* (1869). Still, specific debts to the Sonnets can be difficult to locate, in part because later sonneteers chose not to emulate Shakespeare's stanza but opted, rather, for the Petrarchan format. Meredith departed even further in writing all his sonnets in sixteen-line stanzas. But the sentiments expressed also belong profoundly to Victorian England. Meredith's cycle shows the influence of the realistic novel, Rossetti's a desire for things (and symbols) medieval, and Barrett Browning for feminine deference and religiosity. Her most famous poem, in fact, 'How do I love thee, let me count the ways', transposes lines spoken by Goneril from *King Lear* but now aeriated of duplicity. Tennyson is scandalously closer to sounding passion's darker extremities in the Sonnets in *In Memoriam* when, mourning the loss of Arthur Henry Hallam, he remarks, 'I loved thee, Spirit, and love, nor can / The soul of Shakespeare love thee more' (61.11–12). And Gerard Manley Hopkins strikes a true Shakespearean note of desperation, with comparable multifarious imagery and wordplay, in his 'terrible sonnets', albeit drawn from the drama, not the Sonnets.

Among modern poets Robert Frost stands out, especially because attacks on writing in traditional forms had become *de rigueur*. Frost's sonnets are among the best and most formally varied of any in the 20th century, but love is usually at their centre. An early sonnet, 'Putting in the Seed' (1916), is, in its tightly observed rhyme scheme, more Shakespearean than Shakespeare, an earthy erotic revision of the husbandry motif frequently at work in the early-numbered Shakespeare Sonnets. Given Frost's crafty way of situating himself in relation to tradition, moreover, we might even read the poem as an instance of his slyly shouldering his way through his ancestral and Shakespearean past, gaining a freedom eventually fully realized in 'A Silken Tent' (1942). He spins that late love sonnet out of a single sentence held loosely together by a perfectly formed Shakespearean rhyme scheme.

Shakespeare's Sonnets have also proven to be surprisingly fertile ground for a number of late modernist and post-modernist Anglophone poets on both sides of the Atlantic. Partly because of the familiar place the poems have assumed in the curriculum and the English speaking culture at large, they could be repurposed in a variety of novel directions. Marilyn Hacker, for instance, recounts the yearlong passion of an older person, in this case female, for a younger woman in *Love, Death, and the Changing of the Seasons* (1986). An extended sonnet sequence, it is infused with a keen sense of temporality. Its same-sex situation is explicitly 'seasoned' with borrowings from Shakespeare's Sonnets: Sonnet 73, in particular—the poem serves as an epigraph to the whole while its closing line is the point of departure for her final sonnet—but also Sonnets 2, 97, and 98, which mark crucial turning points in love's saga. Wendy Cope's series of 'Strugnell's Sonnets', in *Making Cocoa for Kingsley Amis*, also published in 1986, belongs to the venerable tradition of English parody, as one might expect in a book with Kingsley Amis's name in the title. It is further lightened by a touch of satire in the invitingly boorish male figure of the speaker, Strugnell, a poet. Each of the seven sonnets grows out of a comically twisted first line from one of Shakespeare's Sonnets. ('The expense of spirits is a crying shame', 'Let me not to the marriage of true swine', etc.)

The sonnet's concern with the familiar Shakespearean theme of perpetuity as well as their status as cultural monuments is more at issue in Jen Bervin's *Nets* (2004). As the abbreviated title in small suggests, the author-editor performs a series of erasures of sixty of Shakespeare's Sonnets in what amounts to a visual confession of the anxiety of Shakespeare's influence. But if the poems can be desecrated and reduced to runic linear fragments, so their words—indeed, seemingly incidental 'function words'—can be recovered and re-used to make an altogether new poem about love, as in the case of Alice Fulton's intricate and moving redaction of Sonnet 87 in 'Peroral', in her recent collection of verse called *Barely Composed* (2015). Carol Ann Duffy's much anthologized love poem, bearing the title of Shakespeare's wife, 'Anne Hathaway', is likewise a perceptive re-casting of the form and subject of the Shakespearean sonnet from an unexpectedly feminist angle. And both Cope and Duffy are among the thirty British poets who produced sonnets in celebration of the 400th anniversary of Shakespeare's death in 2016. We shouldn't regard these later creations as simply paying homage to their great originals; many perform intense acts of reading in the act of re-writing. But it's also hard to imagine any single book of poems by any other author commanding so many 'tongues-to-be your being [to] rehearse' (Sonnet 81).

Chapter 6

A Lover's Complaint and 'The Phoenix and Turtle'

Two outliers

This final chapter will consider two poems that are, in many ways, outliers among Shakespeare's poems and fascinating for being so. *A Lover's Complaint* was originally published at the end of the 1609 edition of Shakespeare's *Sonnets*. Its placement follows a pattern established with Samuel Daniel's *Delia* (1592) of concluding a sonnet sequence with a single work, in Daniel's case the highly popular *Complaint of Rosamond*. 'The Phoenix and Turtle' first appeared in 1601. It was part of an obscure work, *Love's Martyr*, like its title page, a lengthy, rambling poem 'allegorically shadowing the truth of love in the constant fate of the Phoenix and Turtle' by a little-known poet, Robert Chester (Figure 8). The title page also advertised 'poetical essaies' on this topic 'by the best and chiefest of our modern writers'. Shakespeare's name and those of his noteworthy contemporaries—and sometimes rivals—Ben Jonson, George Chapman, and John Marston appear after their respective poems.

Both Shakespeare poems have inspired much commentary, but neither can be said to possess a central place among the author's works. Although readily admitted into the canon by Edmund Malone at the end of the 18th century, *A Lover's Complaint* has often been felt to be un-Shakespearean, its authorship a continuing

LOVES MARTYR:

OR,

ROSALINS COMPLAINT.

Allegorically shadowing the truth of Loue, in the constant Fate of the Phœnix *and Turtle.*

A Poeme enterlaced with much varietie and raritie; *now first translated out of the venerable Italian Torquato* Cæliano, *by* ROBERT CHESTER.

With the true legend of famous King *Arthur*, the last of the nine Worthies, being the first *Essay* of a new *Brytish* Poet: collected out of diuerse Authenticall Records.

To these are added some new compositions, of seuerall moderne Writers whose names are subscribed to their seuerall workes, vpon the first Subiect : viz. the Phœnix *and* Turtle.

Mar: ——— *Mutare dominum non potest liber notus.*

LONDON
Imprinted for E. B.
1601.

8. Robert Chester, *Loves Martyr: or, Rosalins Complaint*, 1601. Title page.

question mark. The poem was recently—and to my mind prematurely—excluded from the 2007 RSC edition of Shakespeare's *Complete Works*. 'The Phoenix and Turtle' is anomalous for a different reason. Its Shakespearean authorship generally accepted, the poem is unlike anything else the poet attempted in both

107

matter and manner. It remains among the most bafflingly beautiful poems in English.

The comparability of these two outliers is also a feature of the enigmatic remoteness of their speakers. Here is how *A Lover's Complaint* begins:

> From off a hill whose concave womb reworded
> A plaintful story from a sist'ring vale,
> My spirits t'attend this double voice accorded,
> And down I laid to list the sad-tuned tale;
> Ere long espied a fickle maid full pale,
> Tearing of papers, breaking rings a-twain,
> Storming her world with sorrow's wind and rain.

In these lines, an unidentified 'I' recalls overhearing a 'plaintful story' by a distraught 'maid'. And here is the beginning of 'The Phoenix and Turtle':

> Let the bird of loudest lay,
> On the sole Arabian tree,
> Herald sad and trumpet be:
> To whose sound chaste wings obey.

In the first case, the anonymous 'I' is a narrator, whose 'spirits' attend to a sad tale by a 'fickle maid full pale' who is also never named and only overheard as a rebounding echo from a distant hill, thus forming a 'double voice'. The second quotation is more concise but no less mysterious in address. Who is this bird being described in the third person? And who or what are the 'chaste wings' obeying its voice? Neither bird will ever be named, although, as with *A Lover's Complaint*, the genre is immediately knowable. The first is a pastoral lament involving a young woman. The second is an obsequy for a pair of birds, who are not identified until line 23 as the Phoenix and Turtle (i.e. a turtle dove, not a tortoise). The conceit of their union is itself unusual, paradoxical, in fact, like so much else in this slender poem. One belongs to the world of myth, the other to nature. The Phoenix, who self-immolates and then, after a time, is re-born from its own ashes, is one of a kind. The turtledove is also legendary for its loyalty to its fellow mate. The belatedly named pair in the poem eventually gave rise in 1807 to a title the poem never had in the original. It is now generally called either 'The Phoenix and the Turtle' or, more compactly, 'The Phoenix and Turtle'.

A Lover's Complaint

A Lover's Complaint narrates the story of a forlorn maid, who was seduced by an experienced courtly wooer and left abandoned in a country hillside, where she voices the story of her woe in slightly over 300 lines of rhyme royal verse. The pastoral setting as well as the strikingly odd, often archaic diction and phrasing—already visible in the first stanza—suggests a link with a tradition of Spenserian 'Complaints' as sounded in *The Ruins of Time* (1591). Some of the poem's unusual images and words seem likewise plucked from the *Prothalamion*, Spenser's marriage poem first published in 1596. The date is important. It suggests that Shakespeare's poem is not the work of an apprentice, as critics once supposed in order to explain its unevenness, but belongs to Shakespeare's middle, perhaps even later years. As a male-authored female complaint, the poem also resembles *The Rape of Lucrece*, but the differences are more telling than the similarities. The 'fickle maid' is not high-born. Her story is not heroic in the generic sense of belonging to the tradition of *de casibus* tragedy, descending from the great accounts of abandoned women in Ovid's *Heroides* popular in Shakespeare's day. Nor is she conventionally heroic. No suicide and no larger political consequences derive from her actions. Although she manifests a degree of agency in seeking to destroy the amatory baubles given to her—rings, letters, and so on (ll. 43–50)—she does not firmly denounce her male seducer, nor, more surprisingly still, is she fully repentant at the poem's end. There are other unusual features to the poem as well. The narrator, an eavesdropper at the outset, is barely present—in sharp contrast to the narrative poems—nor returns at the end to frame the maid's story. And the story the maid tells, which she relates to an unnamed auditor described only as 'a reverend man' (l. 57), involves her adopting the voice of her seducer for over 100 lines, the longest stretch in the poem. She quotes him quoting the responses of other women to his wooing. As such, the poem is a highly reflexive blurring or blending of voices. The title, in fact, can be said to apply to both the seducer, who complains of female resistance, and to the maid whose 'complaint' envelopes his.

Critical responses

Readers who most prize *A Lover's Complaint* often do so for structural, thematic, or ideological reasons. The story it tells is mainly from a woman's point of view, one that is seen to shed retrospective light on the foregoing Sonnets and is in turn illuminated by them. As with many females to whom sonnet sequences are directed, the maid, like the seduced women preceding her in the poem, is the recipient of 'deep-brained sonnets' (l. 209) and other gifts. But in contrast to the sonnet tradition, where the female is usually silent, the genre of the 'Complaint' endows her with a voice. In this mode, she can produce, for instance, a lengthy 'blazon' (ll. 85–105) that includes, in the quoted stanza, a critique of his motives in the couplet:

> His qualities were beauteous as his form,
> For maiden-tongued he was, and thereof free;
> Yet if men moved him, was he such a storm
> As oft 'twixt May and April is to see,
> When winds breathe sweet, unruly though they be.
> His rudeness so with his authorized youth
> Did livery falseness in a pride of truth.

Not only does the maid identify in considerable detail the unnamed giver of the gifts but, in an instance of double-voicing, she also describes the 'tributes' he brings to other women: the 'pallid pearls and rubies red as blood' (l. 198) and other such jewels and 'trophies of affections hot' (l. 218). In his station and appearance, he resembles the somewhat androgynous 'fair youth' of the Sonnets (ll. 85–110); she, as a fallen woman, reminds us of the 'dark lady'. But, in a further twist, he can also be said to be the morally 'darker' of the two in having seduced many women (including a nun!), whereas she, in showing the constancy of her love, can be seen as the fairer of the two.

More subtly still, attending to the structural relationship between the Sonnets and *A Lover's Complaint* helps explain the oddity at the end of the Sonnets, the two so-called 'Anacreontic' sonnets that conclude the collection (Sonnets 153 and 154). Shakespeare was following a convention that appears in Samuel Daniel and other sonneteers of the period, in Shakespeare's case forging a thematic link between the Sonnets and the *Complaint* in the image of Diana's 'seething bath', her 'well', a concentrated metaphor for the various diseases of love explored in both the Sonnets and the *Complaint*.

Some of the most vigorous criticism of *A Lover's Complaint* grapples with how best to understand the maid's estranged circumstances in relation to other sources and traditions, Shakespearean and beyond. To some readers, her plight as a wooed and abandoned woman is reminiscent of Ophelia's situation in *Hamlet*, the unsympathetic treatment she receives suggesting the class difference often found in broadside ballads of the period. To other readers, if the maid fails to live up to the high standards of Lucrece, it may well be because her true genealogy stems from a tradition of 'exculpatory complaints' of the period, in which sympathy for the female victim was a primary feature of the genre. And to still other readers, the 'fickle' maid's refusal to admit fully to her folly at the end of the poem encourages understanding the *Complaint* in light of shifting attitudes toward the practice of confession in Early Modern England.

To further emphasize her status as an outlier and to read her reluctance to repent even more perversely as someone wooed through the medium of other women's words is to highlight the poem's—and the period's—necessarily circuitous participation in unconventional sexuality. (Donne's same-sex poem, 'Sappho to Philaenis', long, but not, of late, considered of dubious authorship, makes an illuminating companion to *A Lover's Complaint*.) More radical still, by concentrating on the subject of sex, it is possible to argue that the real focus of the poem is not on a woman's sexual passion but on the extreme pity she feels for her wooer, someone to whom she willingly sacrifices herself and can imagine doing so again. In this reading, as with many others, the most striking stanza is the last.

> O that infected moisture of his eye;
> O that false fire which in his cheek so glowed;
> O that forced thunder from his heart did fly;
> O that sad breath his spongy lungs bestowed;
> O all that borrowed motion, seeming owed,
> Would yet again betray the fore-betrayed,
> And new pervert a reconcilèd maid.

With its cascading descent of apostrophes, it voices her continuing feelings for the young man and her potential for being seduced yet again, her passion as much rekindled as resolved by medium of the complaint itself. Lucrece, or for that matter the repentant Rosalind of Daniel's poem, Shakespeare's 'fickle maid' most certainly and curiously is not.

The authorship question

And yet—to raise the spectre of authorship—is it clear precisely whom we are hearing in *A Lover's Complaint*? Readers have divided strongly on the vexing matter of the poem's authorship. Discerning work of a highly technical order has analysed the poem's diction, especially with regard to 'rare words', and, from this specific angle, there seems no better candidate for authorship than Shakespeare himself. The 'rare words' in *A Lover's Complaint* appear more frequently in his work than in the work of any of his contemporaries. But it's also true that there remain any number of lines and phrases, stylistic tics, that seem both unusual and awkward and do not appear elsewhere in Shakespeare's writing or at least not in the same quantity, nor in those works of his closest in form and subject to this one, the other narrative poems: flat lines—'to make the weeper laugh, the laugher weep' (ll. 124–5); clichés—'burning blushes', 'weeping water', 'sounding paleness' (ll. 304–5); over-used hyphenated adjectives—'Deep-green em'rald', 'heaven-hued sapphire', 'wit well-blazoned' (ll. 213–17), all appearing in the same stanza; awkward rhymes within stanzas, as in 'hovered' and 'lovered'; and stanzas that conclude not with a bang but a whimper—'For on his visage was in little drawn / What largeness thinks in paradise was sawn' (ll. 90–1).

Is it possible, then, that we are hearing someone else in this poem, perhaps an imitator of Shakespeare imitating Spenser? Or perhaps someone with whom he was collaborating as he occasionally did in writing plays, a fellow actor, for example, as Shakespeare once was while writing his own narrative poems when the plague was around? That is, a person who was thoroughly familiar with his writings, who could 're-word' but not equal the teacher; who at the beginning might recall the first lines of *Lucrece* ('From the besiegèd Ardea all in post, / Bourne by the trustless wings of false desire'), but not quite capture their energy: 'From off a hill whose concave womb reworded / A plaintful story from a sist'ring vale'. To throw out a name from 'a sist'ring vale': might that person even be, say, Aemelia Lanyer? Probably not, but also probably not the prolific John Davies of Hereford either, another candidate championed of late. Better for the debate to continue, though, than to be quashed by the poem's expulsion from the canon.

'The Phoenix and Turtle'

'The Phoenix and Turtle' seems almost everything *A Lover's Complaint* is not: a trim, datable, finely wrought, eulogistic celebration of chastity in only sixty-seven lines, not a round-about tale of multiple seductions. The poem has a clearly marked tripartite structure. The obsequy begins with five stanzas in which avian mourners of 'these dead birds' assemble. The distinctive qualities of 'The Phoenix and Turtle' then form the subject of the longer eight-stanza 'anthem'. The poem concludes with a brief *Threnos*, or lamentation, of another five stanzas that further concentrates their special attributes into a few familiar abstractions: 'Beauty, Truth, and Rarity, / Grace in all simplicity, / Here enclosed, in cinders lie' (ll. 53–5). The poem possesses a near perfect, symmetrical match between the celebration of chaste love and strictness of form and simplicity of diction.

Critical mysteries

Why then has so slender a poem been the subject of so much curiosity? Part of the poem's mystery surrounds the circumstances of its publication. What is this lone poem doing in so unlikely a place as Chester's collection of verse, and how did it get there? Was it perhaps because of the printer, Richard Field, originally from Stratford, who had earlier published Shakespeare's narrative poems and knew a poem by Shakespeare might help Chester's cause? Or did joining a community of other 'modern' poets pique Shakespeare's interest, perhaps out of a sense of rivalry, as we saw in the Sonnets, and because some of his sonnets had been recently purloined and indiscriminately published in *The Passionate Pilgrim*? Or was it because of a connection of some kind stemming from the person to whom *Love's Martyr* is dedicated, the Welsh magnate and courtier Sir John Salusbury, and the theatre, which Salusbury perhaps supported? Questions like these become only more urgent when we recall the singularity of the poem's appearance. None of Shakespeare's other poems seems so unmotivated, not even the Sonnets, and none delimits its amatory subject matter so precisely. But here, in mid-career, the recent author of *Hamlet* and *Troilus and Cressida* suddenly writes a poem on 'married chastity'. A peculiar consummation but one perhaps devoutly to be wished after all the gruelling infidelities in those two dramas. Even Shakespeare might want a holiday from the hothouse of constant play writing on those subjects, and improvising in the company of others on an unusual topic certainly provided one.

With this poem, questions of context inevitably spill over into matters of content. From the late 19th century forward, Chester's volume has prompted a slew of allegorical readings of Shakespeare's poem, some more probable than others. Heraldically minded Elizabethans, for instance, would find it easy to think of their long-lived and unique queen as the Phoenix. There were also plenty of possible Turtles available in 1601. A sampling includes Robert Devereux, the Earl of Essex, a one-time favourite of Elizabeth whose ill-judged rebellion led to his execution; the recently knighted Sir John Salusbury, squire of the body in the royal bedchamber, in need of securing his place as the preferred candidate for Parliament; the English people in general anxious over losing their ageing queen. It's difficult to discount the topical resonances and tremors readers in 1601 might feel, but the many possibilities offered by later critics, often with one rebutting another, also work to undermine the approach itself. Those most alert to the poem's historical complexities have often felt the need to read the poem in a more flexible, less time bound way and to attend to the specific nature of its poetics, the much that is unspecified and that eludes historical events.

In this regard, the poem has important literary antecedents, if not sources, in other bird poems from antiquity and the recent past. Marlowe had translated Ovid's *In mortem psittaci* ('On the Death of a Parrot') in his *Elegies* (*c.*1593); before that, John Skelton had written a bird poem mourning the death of Phillip Sparrow, and Chaucer, 'The Parliament of Fowls'. Shakespeare had also depended on a similar metrical version of what is sometimes called 'beheaded' tetrameter verse of seven syllables in the theatre to produce, among other instances, dirges in both *Much Ado About Nothing* (5.3) and *Cymbeline* (4.2) and the two bird songs, mostly in tetrameter, at the end of *Love's Labour's Lost*. Sidney, too, had used a similar metre to great effect in his much imitated eighth song in *Astrophel and Stella*, whose music Shakespeare's poem is sometimes said to recall. But 'The Phoenix and Turtle' doesn't mourn the death of either a person or a pet, or the dissolution of lovers' bonds. Rather, it eulogizes two birds who possessed exceptional human qualities. In fact, so exceptional are they in their mutual love as to be altogether beyond exemplarity, not only because the likes of which the world wouldn't see again but because the birds, in their unusual condition of married chastity, leave no offspring, a situation that has helped to fuel disagreement over whether the poem should be read optimistically or pessimistically, as celebration or lament.

Poetic mysteries: number there in love was slain

'The Phoenix and Turtle' is not just a mysterious poem, however, with regard to context and sources. It is a mysterious poem by design. It is about love's defeat of Reason, not through the elevation of a Dionysian passion but by exploiting and undermining Reason's logical capacities. The elegantly compact separation of the sacred from the profane that marks the rite of mourning in stanzas 1–5 gives way to an 'anthem' highly indebted to theological discourse not elsewhere found in Shakespeare but reminiscent or strongly anticipatory of the 'metaphysical' verse of John Donne emerging at the end of the 1590s. Written slightly later, Donne's 'The Canonization', with its phoenix-like lovers, was perhaps directly influenced by Shakespeare's poem, thus giving 'The Phoenix and Turtle', in the minds of some critics, an important role in the production of metaphysical verse itself by Donne and his followers.

Part old, part new, song-like yet rigorously scholastic and paradoxical, Shakespeare's poem has an indisputably hybrid quality to it. As the most polymorphic love poet in English, Shakespeare never stopped thinking about how two people do and/or do not become one. That is the great burden of the Sonnets. It is also the motivating impulse behind the narrative poems, to limit ourselves just to the works presented in this study. Venus utterly fails to become one with Adonis; Tarquin unequivocally forces himself on Lucrece; with the poet of the Sonnets representing various scenarios, ranging from the obligations of reproductive sex to the heady marriage of two minds with many possibilities and postures in between. In fact, the more we attempt to enumerate the possibilities, the more innumerable they seem, as does love itself.

'The Phoenix and Turtle' plays on this understanding. Shakespeare offers yet another version of love, but this one concentrates on the absolute mystery whereby two become one. Any stanza from 'the anthem' could be cited as specific proof, so multiple is this truth:

> So they loved as love in twain,
> Had the essence but in one,
> Two distincts, division none:
> Number there in love was slain.
>
> Hearts remote, yet not asunder;
> Distance and no space was seen
> 'Twixt this Turtle and his queen;
> But in them it were a wonder.

So between them love did shine
That the Turtle saw his right
Flaming in the Phoenix' sight;
Either was the other's mine.

Property was thus appalled
That the self was not the same:
Single natures, double name,
Neither two nor one was called.

Reason in itself confounded
Saw division grow together;
To themselves yet either neither,
Simple were so well compounded,

That it cried 'How true a twain
Seemeth this concordant one:
Love hath reason, Reason none,
If what parts can so remain.'

What is highly compressed can be gnomic, especially when the diction becomes suddenly abstract, indeed mathematical, in describing the fusion of two into one that, nonetheless, doesn't obliterate distinctions but respects difference. The pithiness can also almost boggle the mind, as in the phrase 'Either was the other's mine', as can the pun on mind itself, the self now encapsulated in a thought, the thought even including the explosive, military sense of a mine activated by love to produce a mutual flame as unique as the Phoenix' self-combustion. So compact, in fact, is Shakespeare's language that one of its main effects is to produce, as scholastic philosophy often does, nearly endless commentary on its meaning.

Another consequence is that the pressure of paradox invites an intellectual concentration appropriate to the amatory experience as described. For all its potential aridity, there is something wonderfully ludic in Property's puzzlement, and in Reason's outburst against itself. The linking stanza to the final movement, the 'Threnos', is also pointedly over the top, presenting 'The Phoenix and the dove' as 'Co-supremes and stars of love, / As chorus to their tragic scene'. They're not Hollywood material, of course, but reference to the stage reminds us of just who the author of the poem is, and we almost expect from this advertisement a finish in bold letters. But in this poem decorum rules, perfectly. The 'Threnos' employs, rather, a reduction in scale, from quatrains to tercets. In doing so, the poem doesn't ask for applause from the many but invites only those 'who are either true or fair' to mourn what is now lost and 'to sigh a prayer'. In the poem's mysterious beginning lies its incantatory end. The chastened reader joins the other 'chaste wings' as a participant in this mysterious rite:

> Beauty, Truth, and Rarity,
> Grace in all simplicity,
> Here enclosed in cinders lie.
>
> Death is now the Phoenix' nest,
> And the Turtle's loyal breast
> To eternity doth rest.
>
> Leaving no posterity,
> 'Twas not their infirmity:
> It was married chastity.
>
> Truth may seem, but cannot be;
> Beauty brag, but 'tis not she:
> Truth and Beauty burièd be.
>
> To this urn let those repair
> That are either true or fair:
> For these dead birds sigh a prayer.

A brief finale indeed

Once heard, read, or spoken, 'The Phoenix and Turtle' is rarely forgotten. It's not Shakespeare's last word, but sometimes it is understandably treated as such. England's poet laureate, Ted

Hughes, concluded his compilation of *The Essential Shakespeare* (1971; revised 1991) with this poem, appearing after Prospero's famous speech beginning, 'Our revels now are ended'. More memorable still, near the end of his life, Wallace Stevens recalled the poem's remote setting and imagery in his gorgeously delphic poem 'Of Mere Being'. There is something definitive about Shakespeare's hard, beautiful poem. Language is pushed to the extreme until dramatic speech and lyric fold into each other—spoken anthem into airy 'sigh'. The semantic value of language is still intact, but just barely. Beyond this threshold, marked by a sigh, only song remains, or seems to, as in Ariel's sonorous 'Full fathom five' from *The Tempest* or in the brisk cadences of 'Who is Sylvia', extracted from *The Two Gentlemen of Verona* and later set to music by Franz Schubert. But this is a subject also beyond the bounds of this book. In Shakespeare, the fulfilment of song belongs to the theatre—to the stage, not the page.

Timeline: England

1601	'The Phoenix and Turtle' published as part of Robert Chester's *Love's Martyr*
1603	Elizabeth dies; James VI of Scotland becomes King James I of England
1609	*SHAKE-SPEARES SONNETS* published, with *A Lover's Complaint*
1616	Shakespeare dies; Jonson's *Works* published
1623	Shakespeare's *Works* published; includes only the plays
1640	John Benson publishes *Poems: Written by Wil. Sh.*
1790	Edmond Malone (ed.), *Plays and Poems of William Shakespeare*

References

All quotations from Shakespeare's poems are from Colin Burrow (ed.), *The Complete Sonnets and Poems* (Oxford University Press, 2002).

Chapter 1: Poet and playwright

Emerson quotation, from Hyder Edward Rollins (ed.), *The Sonnets* (vol. II; J. B. Lippincott, 1944), 369.

On poems attributed to Shakespeare, see Colin Burrow, *The Complete Sonnets and Poems* (Oxford University Press, 2002), 146–58.

'woodnotes wild', from John Milton, 'L'Allegro', line 135.

James Longenbach, 'The sound of Shakespeare thinking', in Jonathan F. S. Post (ed.), *The Oxford Handbook of Shakespeare's Poetry* (Oxford University Press, 2013), 618–30.

Allen Ginsberg's speculations, from Theodore Leinwand, *The Great William: Writers Reading Shakespeare* (University of Chicago Press, 2016), 148.

Numerical figures, from Sasha Roberts, *Reading Shakespeare's Poems in Early Modern England* (Palgrave Macmillan, 2003), 2–3, 42–3, 83–101.

Chapter 2: *Venus and Adonis*

Plague death numbers, as reported in Colin Burrow, *The Complete Sonnets and Poems* (Oxford University Press, 2002), 202.

Wriothesley material, from Park Honan, 'Wriothesley, Henry, third earl of Southampton (1573–1624)', *Oxford Dictionary of National Biography* (Oxford University Press, 2004).

'wiser sort', from G. Blakemore Evans (ed.), *The Riverside Shakespeare* (Houghton Mifflin, 1974), 1840.

'titillating responses', from Sasha Roberts, *Reading Shakespeare's Poems in Early Modern England* (Palgrave Macmillan, 2003), 46.

Symonds quote, from Subha Mukherji, 'Outgrowing Adonis, outgrowing Ovid: the disorienting narrative of *Venus and Adonis*', in Jonathan F. S. Post (ed.), *The Oxford Handbook of Shakespeare's Poetry* (Oxford University Press, 2013), 397.

'Sixain', from Frank Whigham and Wayne A. Rebhorn (eds), *The Art of English Poesy by George Puttenham: A Critical Edition* (Cornell University Press, 2007), 155.

'first critic to recognize', in reference to S. T. Coleridge, 'Lectures on literature, 1808–1819', in R. A. Foakes (ed.), *Collected Works* (vol. 5.1; Princeton University Press, 1987).

'This magical simile', from Colin Burrow, *The Complete Sonnets and Poems* (Oxford University Press, 2002), 218.

'Male body "rooting" male body', from Richard Rambuss, 'What it feels like for a boy: Shakespeare's *Venus and Adonis*', in Richard Dutton and Jean Howard (eds), *A Companion to Shakespeare's Works: Poems, Problem Comedies, Late Plays* (vol. 4; Blackwell, 2003), 249.

Chapter 3: *The Rape of Lucrece*

'The wiser sort', from G. Blakemore Evans (ed.), *The Riverside Shakespeare* (Houghton Mifflin, 1974), 1840.

'more prestigious octavo format', from Lukas Erne, *Shakespeare and the Book Trade* (Cambridge University Press, 2013), 148.

'sage sayer', from Frank Whigham and Wayne A. Rebhorn (eds), *The Art of English Poesy by George Puttenham: A Critical Edition* (Cornell University Press, 2007), 321.

Citation information, from Sasha Roberts, *Reading Shakespeare's Poems in Early Modern England* (Palgrave Macmillan, 2003), 130–1.

'exhaustively discussed poems', from Jonathan Crewe, 'The narrative poems', in Stephen Orgel and A. R. Braunmuller (eds), *The Complete Pelican Shakespeare* (Penguin, 2002), 7.

'feminist philosophers', from A. W. Eaton, 'What's wrong with the female nude', in Hans Maes and Jerrold Levinson (eds), *Art and Pornography: Philosophical Essays* (Oxford University Press, 2012), 296.

'modest eloquence', from Joshua Scodel, 'Shame, love, fear, and pride in *The Rape of Lucrece*', in Jonathan F. S. Post (ed.), *The Oxford Handbook of Shakespeare's Poetry* (Oxford University Press, 2013), 413–30.

'a charge of adultery', from Lorna Hutson, *Circumstantial Shakespeare* (Oxford University Press, 2015), 88.

'traumatic event', from Cathy Caruth, *Unclaimed Experience: Trauma, Narrative, and History* (The Johns Hopkins University Press, 1996), 11.

Chapter 4: On first looking into Shakespeare's *Sonnets*

Dating evidence of Sonnets, as reported by Colin Burrow, *The Complete Sonnets and Poems* (Oxford University Press, 2002), 104–6.

'love was the one theme', from Don Paterson, *Reading Shakespeare's Sonnets: A New Commentary* (Faber, 2010), 492.

Allen Ginsberg's reaction, from Theodore Leinwand, *The Great William: Writers Reading Shakespeare* (University of Chicago Press, 2016), 149.

'there for itself', from Clive James, *Poetry Notebook: Reflection on the Intensity of Language* (Liveright, 2014), 38.

Book XV, *Ovid's Metamorphoses: The Arthur Golding Translation* (Macmillan, 1965; rpt John Dry, 2000), 403.

Chapter 5: Further patterns and irruptions in the *Sonnets*

'Real time', from Jonathan Culler, *Theory of the Lyric* (Harvard University Press, 2015), 36–7.

Keats quotation, from Hyder Edward Rollins (ed.), *The Sonnets* (vol. II; J. B. Lippincott, 1944), 350.

'excellent throughout', from W. H. Auden's introduction to *The Sonnets and Narrative Poems: The Complete Nondramatic Poetry*, ed. William Burto (Signet Classics, 1964; rpt. 1999), p. xliv.

Victorian poetry material, condensed from Herbert F. Tucker, 'Shakespearean being: the Victorian bard', in Jonathan F. S. Post (ed.), *The Oxford Handbook of Shakespeare's Poetry* (Oxford University Press, 2013), 582–98.

James Hirsh, 'Covert appropriations of Shakespeare', *Papers on Language and Literature* 43(1) (Winter, 2007), 45–67.

Thirty British poets, in Hannah Crawforth and Elizabeth Scott-Baumann (eds), *On Shakespeare's Sonnets: A Poets' Celebration* (Arden, 2016).

Chapter 6: *A Lover's Complaint* and 'The Phoenix and Turtle'

A Lover's Complaint

Dating evidence:

MacDonald P. Jackson, 'Echoes of Spenser's *Prothalamion* as evidence against an early date for Shakespeare's *A Lover's Complaint*', *Notes and Queries* 235 (1990), 180–2.

Critical responses:

John Kerrigan, *The Sonnets and A Lover's Complaint* (Penguin, 1986), 1–18.

Katherine Duncan-Jones, *Shakespeare's Sonnets* (Arden, 2010), 89–96.

Katharine A. Craik, 'Poetry and compassion in Shakespeare's "A Lover's Complaint"', in Jonathan F. S. Post (ed.), *The Oxford Handbook of Shakespeare's Poetry* (Oxford University Press, 2013), 522–39.

John Roe, 'Unfinished business: *A Lover's Complaint*, and *Hamlet*, *Romeo and Juliet*, and *The Rape of Lucrece*', in Shirley Sharon-Zisser (ed.), *Critical Essays on Shakespeare's A Lover's Complaint* (Ashgate, 2006), 109–20.

Ilona Bell, 'Shakespeare's exculpatory complaint', in Shirley Sharon-Zisser (ed.), *Critical Essays on Shakespeare's A Lover's Complaint* (Ashgate, 2006), 91–107.

Paul Stegner, 'A reconciled maid: *A Lover's Complaint* and confessional practices in early modern England', in Shirley Sharon-Zisser (ed.), *Critical Essays on Shakespeare's A Lover's Complaint* (Ashgate, 2006), 79–90.

Catherine Bates, *Masculinity, Gender and Identity in the English Renaissance Lyric* (Cambridge University Press, 2007).

Melissa Sanchez, 'The poetics of feminine subjectivity in Shakespeare's Sonnets and *A Lover's Complaint*', in Jonathan F. S. Post (ed.), *The Oxford Handbook of Shakespeare's Poetry* (Oxford University Press, 2013), 505–21.

Authorship question:

Brian Vickers, *Shakespeare, A Lover's Complaint, and John Davies of Hereford* (Cambridge University Press, 2007).

MacDonald P. Jackson, 'The authorship of *A Lover's Complaint*: a new approach to the problem', *Papers. Bibliographical Society of America* 102(3) (September, 2008), 285–313.

'The Phoenix and Turtle'

Critical positions, summarized in James P. Bednarz, *Shakespeare and the Truth of Love: The Mystery of 'The Phoenix and Turtle'* (Palgrave Macmillan, 2012).

Ted Hughes, *The Essential Shakespeare* (1971; revised Ecco Press, 1991).

Further reading

Editions of poems and sonnets

Stephen Booth, *Shakespeare's Sonnets* (Yale University Press, 1977).

Colin Burrow, *The Complete Sonnets and Poems* (Oxford University Press, 2002).

Katherine Duncan-Jones, *Shakespeare's Sonnets* (Arden, 1997).

Katherine Duncan-Jones and Henry Woudhuysen (eds), *Shakespeare's Poems: Venus and Adonis, The Rape of Lucrece and The Shorter Poems* (Arden, 2007).

G. Blakemore Evans, *Shakespeare's Sonnets* (Cambridge University Press, 1996, 2006).

John Kerrigan, *The Sonnets* and *A Lover's Complaint* (Penguin, 1986).

Raphael Lyne and Cathy Shrank, *The Complete Poems of Shakespeare* (Routledge, forthcoming 2017).

John Roe, *Poems: Venus and Adonis, The Rape of Lucrece, The Phoenix and the Turtle, The Passionate Pilgrim, A Lover's Complaint* (Cambridge University Press, 1992).

General criticism

Patrick Cheney (ed.), *The Cambridge Companion to Shakespeare's Poetry* (Cambridge University Press, 2007).

A. D. Cousins, *Shakespeare's Sonnets and Narrative Poems* (Longman, 2000).

Heather Dubrow, *Captive Victors: Shakespeare's Narrative Poems and the Sonnets* (Cornell University Press, 1987).

Peter Hyland, *An Introduction to Shakespeare's Poems* (Palgrave Macmillan, 2003).

Dennis Kay, *William Shakespeare: Sonnets and Poems* (Twayne, 1998).

John Kerrigan, 'Shakespeare's Poems', in Margareta de Grazia and Stanley Wells (eds), *The Cambridge Companion to Shakespeare* (Cambridge University Press, 2001).

Stephen Orgel and Sean Keileen (eds), *Shakespeare's Poems* (Garland, 1999).

Jonathan F. S. Post (ed.), *The Oxford Handbook of Shakespeare's Poetry* (Oxford University Press, 2013).

Sasha Roberts, *Reading Shakespeare's Poems in Early Modern England* (Palgrave Macmillan, 2003).

Michael Schoenfeldt, *The Cambridge Introduction to Shakespeare's Poetry* (Cambridge University Press, 2010).

Stanley Wells, *Shakespeare, Sex and Love* (Oxford University Press, 2010).

Chapter 1: Poet and playwright

Patrick Cheney, *Shakespeare, National Poet-Playwright* (Cambridge University Press, 2004).

Lukas Erne, *Shakespeare as Literary Dramatist* (Cambridge University Press, 2003; 2nd edn, 2013).

Lukas Erne, *Shakespeare and the Book Trade* (Cambridge, 2013).

Neil Rhodes, *Shakespeare and the Origins of English* (Oxford University Press, 2004).

Charlotte Scott, *Shakespeare and the Idea of the Book* (Oxford University Press, 2007).

George T. Wright, *Shakespeare's Metrical Art* (University of California Press, 1988).

Chapter 2: *Venus and Adonis*

Jonathan Bate, *Shakespeare and Ovid* (Oxford University Press, 1993).

Colin Burrow, *Shakespeare and Classical Antiquity* (Oxford University Press, 2013).

Paul Edmondson, 'The narrative poetry of Marlowe and Shakespeare', in Michael O'Neill (ed.), *The Cambridge History of English Poetry* (Cambridge University Press, 2010).

Clark Hulse, *Metamorphic Verse: The Elizabethan Minor Epic* (Princeton University Press, 1981).

Philip C. Kolin (ed.), *Venus and Adonis: Critical Essays* (Garland, 1997).

Anthony Mortimer, *Variable Passions: A Reading of Shakespeare's Venus and Adonis* (AMS Press, 2000).

Daniel D. Moss, *The Ovidian Vogue: Literary Fashion and Imitative Practice in Late Elizabethan England* (University of Toronto Press, 2014).

John Mulryan and Steven Brown (eds), *Natali Conti's Mythologiae* (2 vols; Center for Medieval and Renaissance Studies, 2006).

John Frederick Nims (ed.), *Ovid's Metamorphoses: The Arthur Golding Translation, 1567* (Macmillan, 1965; rpt Paul Dry Books, 2000).

Shormishtha Panja, '"Those lips that love's own hand did make": Anne Hathaway and Shakespeare's *Venus and Adonis*', in R. S. Desai (ed.), *Shakespeare the Man: New Decipherings* (Fairleigh Dickinson University Press, 2014).

Chapter 3: *The Rape of Lucrece*

Catherine Belsey, 'Tarquin dispossessed: expropriation and consent in *The Rape of Lucrece*', *Shakespeare Quarterly* 53 (Fall, 2001), 315–35.

Alison A. Chapman, 'Lucrece's time', *Shakespeare Quarterly* 64 (Summer, 2013), 165–87.

Ian Donaldson, *The Rapes of Lucretia: A Myth and its Transformations* (Oxford University Press, 1982).

James A. W. Heffernan, *Museum of Words: The Poetics of Ekphrasis from Homer to Ashbery* (University of Chicago Press, 1993).

Jeffrey Paxton Hehmeyer, 'Heralding the commonplace: authorship, voice, and the commonplace in Shakespeare's *Rape of Lucrece*', *Shakespeare Quarterly* 64 (Summer, 2013), 139–64.

Lorna Hutson, *Circumstantial Shakespeare* (Oxford University Press, 2015).

Stephanie H. Jed, *Chaste Thinking: The Rape of Lucretia and the Birth of Humanism* (Indiana University Press, 1989).

Coppélia Kahn, *Roman Shakespeare: Warriors, Wounds and Women* (Routledge, 1997).

John Kerrigan, *Motives of Woe: Shakespeare and 'Female Complaint', a Critical Anthology* (Oxford University Press, 1991).

John Kerrigan, *Shakespeare's Binding Language* (Oxford University Press, 2016).

Joshua Scodel, 'Shame, love, fear, and pride in *The Rape of Lucrece*', in Jonathan F. S. Post (ed.), *The Oxford Handbook of Shakespeare's Poetry* (Oxford University Press, 2013), 413–30.

Nancy Vickers, '"The blazon of sweet beauty's best": Shakespeare's *Lucrece*', in Patricia Parker and Geoffrey Hartman (eds), *Shakespeare and the Question of Theory* (Methuen, 1985), 95–115.

William P. Weaver, '"O teach me how to make mine own excuse": forensic performance in *Lucrece*', *Shakespeare Quarterly* 59 (Winter, 2008), 421–49.

Chapter 4: On first looking into Shakespeare's *Sonnets*

Stephen Booth, *An Essay on Shakespeare's Sonnets* (Yale University Press, 1968).

Brian Boyd, *Why Lyrics Last: Evolution, Cognition, and Shakespeare's Sonnets* (Harvard University Press, 2012).

Colin Burrow, 'Editing the Sonnets', in Michael Schoenfeldt (ed.), *A Companion to Shakespeare's Sonnets* (Blackwell, 2007).

Dympna Callahan, *Shakespeare's Sonnets* (Blackwell, 2007).

A. D. Cousins and Peter Howarth (eds), *The Cambridge Companion to the Sonnet* (Cambridge University Press, 2011).

Paul Edmondson and Stanley Wells, *Shakespeare's Sonnets* (Oxford University Press, 2004).

Barbara Everett, 'Shakespeare and the Elizabethan Sonnet', *London Review of Books*, 8 May 2008.

Joseph Pequigney, *Such is My Love: A Study of Shakespeare's Sonnets* (University of Chicago Press, 1985).

Jonathan F. S. Post (ed.), *The Oxford Handbook of Shakespeare's Poetry* (Oxford University Press, 2013).

James Schiffer (ed.), *Shakespeare's Sonnets: Critical Essays* (Garland, 1999).

Michael Schoenfeldt (ed.), *A Companion to Shakespeare's Sonnets* (Blackwell, 2007).

Michael R. J. Spiller, *The Development of the Sonnet: An Introduction* (Routledge, 1992).

Ramie Targoff, *Posthumous Love: Eros and the Afterlife in Renaissance England* (University of Chicago Press, 2014).

Helen Vendler, *The Art of Shakespeare's Sonnets* (Harvard University Press, 1997).

Chapter 5: Further patterns and irruptions in the *Sonnets*

Stephen Burt and David Mikics, *The Art of the Sonnet* (Harvard University Press, 2010).

Neil Corcoran, *Shakespeare and the Modern Poet* (Cambridge University Press, 2012).

Hannah Crawforth, Elizabeth Scott-Baumann, and Clare Whitehead (eds), *The Sonnets: The State of Play* (Arden, 2017).

Roland Greene, *Post-Petrarchism: Origins and Innovations of the Western Lyric Sequence* (Princeton University Press, 1991).

Jeff Hilson (ed.), *The Reality Street Book of Sonnets* (Reality Street Editions, 2008).

J. B. Leishman, *Themes and Variations in Shakespeare's Sonnets* (2nd edn; Hutchinson University Library, 1961).

Chapter 6: *A Lover's Complaint* and 'The Phoenix and Turtle'

A Lover's Complaint

Ilona Bell, '"That which thou hast done": Shakespeare's Sonnets and "A Lover's Complaint"', in James Schiffer (ed.), *Shakespeare's Sonnets: Critical Essays* (Garland, 1999), 455–74.

Katherine A. Craik, 'Shakespeare's *A Lover's Complaint* and early modern criminal confession', *Shakespeare Quarterly* 53, 4 (2002): 437–59.

Margaret Healy, *Shakespeare, Alchemy and the Creative Imagination: The Sonnets and A Lover's Complaint* (Cambridge University Press, 2011).

J. M. Mackail, 'A Lover's Complaint', *Essays and Studies* 3 (1912), 51–70.

Shirley Sharon-Zisser (ed.), *Critical Essays on Shakespeare's A Lover's Complaint* (Ashgate, 2006).

Brian Vickers, *Shakespeare, A Lover's Complaint, and John Davies of Hereford* (Cambridge University Press, 2007).

Brian Vickers, 'No Shakespeare to be found', *Times Literary Supplement* 3 April 2015.

'The Phoenix and Turtle'

James P. Bednarz, *Shakespeare and the Truth of Love: The Mystery of 'The Phoenix and Turtle'* (Palgrave Macmillan, 2012).

Carleton Brown (ed.), *Poems by Sir John Sulusbury and Robert Chester*, Early English Texts Society, extra series 113 (Oxford University Press, 1914).

H. Neville Davies, '"The Phoenix and the Turtle": requiem and rite', *Review of English Studies* 46 (1995), 525–9.

Lynn Enterline, '"The Phoenix and the Turtle," Renaissance elegies and the language of grief', in Andrew Hadfield and Garrett A. Sullivan, Jr. (eds), *Early Modern English Poetry: A Critical Companion* (Oxford University Press, 2007), 147–59.

Barbara Everett, 'Set upon a golden bough to sing: Shakespeare's debt to Sidney in "The Phoenix and Turtle"', *Times Literary Supplement* 16 February 2001, 13–15.

Anthea Hume, '*Love's Martyr*, "The Phoenix and the Turtle", and the aftermath of the Essex Rebellion', *Review of English Studies*, 40 (1989), 48–71.

John Kerrigan, 'Shakespeare, Elegy and Epitaph, 1557–1640', in Jonathan F. S. Post (ed.), *The Oxford Handbook of Shakespeare's Poetry* (Oxford University Press, 2013), 225–44.

John Kerrigan, 'Reading "The Phoenix and Turtle"', in Jonathan F. S. Post (ed.), *The Oxford Handbook of Shakespeare's Poetry* (Oxford University Press, 2013), 540–59.

John Klause, '"The Phoenix and Turtle" in its time', in Thomas Moisan and Douglas Bruster (eds), *In the Company of Shakespeare* (Fairleigh Dickinson University Press, 2002), 206–30.

G. Wilson Knight, *The Mutual Flame: On Shakespeare's Sonnets and the Phoenix and the Turtle* (Methuen, 1955).

William Matchett, *The Phoenix and the Turtle: Shakespeare's Poem and Chester's Loves Martyr* (Mouton, 1965).

Index

ONLINE CATALOGUE
A Very Short Introduction

Our online catalogue is designed to make it easy to find your ideal Very Short Introduction. View the entire collection by subject area, watch author videos, read sample chapters, and download reading guides.

http://fds.oup.com/www.oup.co.uk/general/vsi/index.html

SOCIAL MEDIA
Very Short Introduction

Join our community
www.oup.com/vsi

- Join us online at the official Very Short Introductions Facebook page.
- Access the thoughts and musings of our authors with our online blog.
- Sign up for our monthly e-newsletter to receive information on all new titles publishing that month.
- Browse the full range of Very Short Introductions online.
- Read extracts from the Introductions for free.
- Visit our library of Reading Guides. These guides, written by our expert authors will help you to question again, why you think what you think.
- If you are a teacher or lecturer you can order inspection copies quickly and simply via our website.